CRITICAL THINKING AND PROBLEM SOLVING:

ADVANCED STRATEGIES AND REASONING SKILLS TO INCREASE YOUR DECISION MAKING. A SYSTEMATIC APPROACH TO MASTER LOGIC, AVOID MISTAKES AND BE A CREATIVE PROBLEM SOLVER.

© **Copyright 2020 - All rights reserved**

The content contained within this book may not be reproduced, duplicated or transmitted without direct written permission from the author or the publisher.

Under no circumstances will any blame or legal responsibility be held against the publisher, or author, for any damages, reparation, or monetary loss due to the information contained within this book. Either directly or indirectly.

Legal Notice:

This book is copyright protected. This book is only for personal use. You cannot amend, distribute, sell, use, quote or paraphrase any part, or the content within this book, without the consent of the author or publisher.

Disclaimer Notice:

Please note the information contained within this document is for educational and entertainment purposes only. All effort has been executed to present accurate, up to date, and reliable, complete information. No warranties of any kind are declared or implied. Readers acknowledge that the author is not engaging in the rendering of legal, financial, medical or professional advice. The content within this book has been derived from various sources. Please consult a licensed professional before attempting any techniques outlined in this book.

By reading this document, the reader agrees that under no circumstances is the author responsible for any losses, direct or indirect, which are incurred as a result of the use of information contained within this document, including, but not limited to, — errors, omissions, or inaccuracies.

Table of Contents

Introduction

Chapter 1 What is Critical Thinking and Problem Solving?

Chapter 2 Build Your Problem Solving Skills

Chapter 3 A Portrait of the Critical and Not-So-Critical Thinkers

Chapter4 Critical thinking: skills and competencies

Chapter 5 Logical Thinking: Facts and Logic

Chapter 6 Making Better Decisions

Chapter 7 Use of Critical Thinking to Tackle Challenges

Chapter 8 Win An Argument Every Time

Chapter 9 Critical Thinking Writing: 4 Steps For Perfect Critical Thinking Writing And Evaluation

Chapter 10 Critical Thinking: Obstacles

Problem Solving Exercises to Boost Critical Thinking Skills

Conclusion

Introduction

Problem solving is a term that every human being might have come across on multiple occasions. Everybody states that a manager or a supervisor has to be a master at problem solving. But this is not true! Every human being faces multiple problems in life that he must try to solve. For instance, a housewife has to plan the expenditure for her house carefully. If she finds that she is running short of finances, she must work backward and see how she can overcome the problem while purchasing the same amount of products for her house.

The process of problem solving is not relevant only to human beings. It could be related to most living beings. It was found that there are cats living in the arctic region. Its climate is terribly cold and there is barely any life in the region. There are cats in the region though! Surprising is it not? These cats are lean because their body burns the fat to keep it warm. It cannot last forever without food. There are rabbits in the arctic too. These rabbits are food for the cats. The cat cannot chase the rabbit all over the region. It cannot lose all of its energy in chasing a rabbit that it might not catch. The cat actually analyzes the situation and checks on whether or not it should chase the rabbit. It takes into consideration the distance between the rabbit and itself. If it feels that it can chase the rabbit and catch it, it goes on its hunt.

This is a classic example of problem solving. The problem at hand here is whether or not the cat must hunt for the rabbit. The cat uses the basics of physics in order to obtain a solution. The answer is very simple – yes or no. It is the method through which the answer is obtained that is problem solving!

Using critical thinking techniques allows you to take apart complex problems and understand each element, as well as the effects of your ideas on the problem. Thinking critically can help you when it comes to problem solving.

Most of us can recall from our days in school that a lot of learning once depended on rote memorization. However, when it comes to solving problems, this approach can be a problem. For, in order to solve a problem, we need not just know facts and information, but be able to apply them as related to a situation. This is where critical thinking ability. Comes in. Here is a step-by-step view of critical thinking as it applies to problem solving.

Step 1: Identify the Problem

Well, does it seem surprising that we are starting with this step? This is a simple, yet a crucial step. Think about all the time, energy and resources that we end up dedicating towards problems that don't necessarily need all that attention. Ask yourself a simple question "Is this the right problem to solve?"

More often than not, the usual approach towards solving a problem happens to be reactive. We wait for a problem to arise before thinking of a solution. The first step towards practical problem solving is that you should start being proactive. Find a problem and address it before it can ever arise. Look at all the likely issues that might come up and go about fixing them one after the other.

In order to attempt to solve a problem, you must know whether there really is a problem. This means, taking the time to look at a situation and see whether it is a problem that is worth your time and effort to rectify, or whether there has just been some kind of misunderstanding. When you do locate a problem, you need to identify what exactly it is in detailed and specific terms.

Step 2: Define and Analyze the Problem

This might seem like a very simple thing to do. But like the previous step, this is very important, and you shouldn't skip it. This is, in fact, the key to solve problems efficiently. By combining problems that are valuable to solve and then defining what you are trying to solve, will dramatically help in improving your problem-solving efficiency. Attitude is the key to determining a problem. Try to look for an opportunity in every hurdle you are faced with. Look for the silver lining. This is very important, and it helps you in defining the problem in such a manner that it will help you in focusing on the potential that's available in every situation you come across. Start starving your problems and start feeding all the opportunities you have. Well, you might not see it right away, but every problem is a learning opportunity. When you stop thinking of a problem as an obstacle and instead view it as an opportunity, you will be able to deal with it effectively. So, try framing your problem with a positive attitude, and it will not seem dreadful anymore.

Once you know what the problem is, look at it from many different points of view. This will help you to answer questions such as: Can it be solved? Will you be able to solve it alone or will you need the help of others? Is the problem real, or is it only being perceived in that way?

Analysis comprises of the process of discovering facts and finding out all the relevant information about the situation that you are in. You can even make a checklist of different bits of information that you will require and then go about collecting the same. You will need to dig deep and try to analyze what the problem is and isn't. A critical aspect of this step is to make sure that you involve the right people. You can make use of these three simple questions while selecting the people who can be brought on board for helping you solve the problem.

• Who knows? Who are all the people who know about the situation and have information or something of value to contribute?

• Who cares? Who are all those who would care if something is being done to rectify the problem on hand?

• Who can? Who can help you in finding a solution?

These questions are quite fundamental and can come in handy when you are trying to identify all those who can help you in solving a problem. Analysis often needs a detailed examination of a given situation, and this step shouldn't be skipped at any cost. If you don't analyze a situation thoroughly, you never know what it is and what it isn't. When you don't have this basic information, it does become quite difficult to think of an ideal solution.

Step 3: Brainstorm and Develop Possibilities

In this step, you will review your options as far as solutions to the problem. Every problem can be solved in more than one way. Brainstorm a list with as many solutions that you can think of, making a note of whatever comes to mind. Then narrow your list down to the best and most appropriate possible solutions.

Once you have understood the problem that has to be solved, the next step is to take some time and come up with creative solutions for the problem. It is essential not just to acknowledge the ideas that you come up with, but also the ideas that others put forward. You cannot be a good leader if you don't listen to what others also have to say. You will first need to find the right problem to solve and then think of all the opportunities that such a problem can create. But how exactly will you be able to focus on these opportunities? There will be more than one solution to solve a problem. The idea of this step is to get you to brainstorm on your own or with others to come up with different possibilities. There will always be plenty of alternatives to choose from. It is an important skill to understand the various alternatives that are at your disposal.

Step 4: Decide on a Solution

The next step is to find the best solution for the problem on hand. Now that you have multiple alternatives to choose from, you need to pick one solution and get started with it. It might seem slightly overwhelming when you have different options to choose from, and that's why you need to think about this step carefully. There will be various pros and cons of selecting a particular method. There will be specific constraints that you should take into consideration, and all the likely solutions should be thoroughly evaluated. There are three simple steps that you can follow while selecting a solution.

The first step is to gauge the operational validity it offers. Are you capable of acting on this idea or is it just something that you

talk about? Will you be able to do something immediately for bringing in the future you truly desire? Can this solution be implemented efficiently? The second step is to check its economic validity. Certain solutions are good, but then when you start looking at their economic viability, it defeats the purpose of even trying to solve the problem. The investment you are making for solving a problem shouldn't be greater than the result you are expecting. If this isn't the case, then you should certainly evaluate other solutions. The third step is to think about the personal commitment you will need to make. Do you honestly believe that this idea will work and can you vouch for its viability?

Take some time and think about these questions. All the alternatives wouldn't answer all the three questions. If you find a solution that answers the three questions positively, then you have your final solution that needs to be implemented.

Take another look at your list of possible solutions and take your time in deciding which one of them will work best for the problem that you are dealing with.

Step 5: Take Action

Now that you have carefully reviewed the problem and decided on a solution, it is time to put your plan into action.

This is the most crucial step. If you don't execute an idea, then there is no point in even thinking about solving a problem. However, before you implement a particular idea, make sure that you have carefully defined the problem and the outcome you desire, the problem has been thoroughly analyzed, all the information that you will need is at your disposal, and you have indeed opted for the best course of action that's available to you. If the idea you have zeroed in on doesn't answer any of the above points in the affirmative, then retrace your steps and make the necessary changes.

Step 6: Evaluate and Learn

When you are done executing all the steps, you will need to evaluate the work that's been done. Check if the desired results have been achieved. If not, then check what went wrong. Make a list of all the things that you can improve on the next time around. Every opportunity to solve a problem will teach you something. Be open to learning and evaluate it all yourself.

Make use of these simple steps for solving all the problems that you will come across.

Problem solving is one of those things that we do a million times a day without even realizing it. It's only when the very tough problems arise that we begin to stress out. However, just like every other process, there is a mental model that can help you through this. The first of those is the inversion mental model. It's a model that can be used alone or that can be combined with other models through your problem-solving process.

Inversion Mental Model

The inversion mental model, though listed under the problem-solving category, is actually one of the most powerful tools in the mental model toolbox. The inversion method blossomed from the mathematical elements of German mathematician Carl Gustav Jacob Jacobi, who worked on elliptical functions. He would solve his problems with the following strategy: man muss immer umkehren. This means "invert, always invert."

From that thought sprung the inversion mental model used to show that you can't just look at your problems in one manner. In order to get the entire scope of a project, you have to look at it forward and backward. When you invert someone, it forces your mind to see it in a different light and to uncover truths about the problem or project you have at hand. Obviously, thinking about the exact opposite of the problem doesn't really come naturally to us, but some of the most brilliant people in history have solved problems doing just that.

Don't expect to always invert your problems and magically find the answers; it doesn't quite work like that. What it will do is give you another perspective to draw from, which will allow you to see problematic areas as well as clues toward the path you need to take in order to break through those problems.

Occam's Razor

Simply put, Occam's razor says that the simplest of answers is always the correct answer. We need to stop racking our brains attempting to find complex solutions to problems and begin focusing on what actually works for it. This mental model is great for solving problems, but it is also good for drawing initial conclusions before the bulk of the facts or before certain information is brought into the picture.

Arthur Conan Doyle's, "Sherlock Holmes", explained Occam's razor. He asserted that if you get rid of the impossible, the thing that remains - no matter how ridiculous, impossible, or even improbable - must be the truth.

Scientifically, there have been studies that have proven the theory of Occam's razor. The principle of minimum energy, a sector of the second law of thermodynamics, simply finds that whenever it's possible, the least amount of energy is used. This concept is utilized in science, business, project management, problem solving, and many more fields.

William of Ockham, a friar, philosopher, and theologian in the 14th century, didn't exactly theorize Occam's razor, but he was known for deducing, which helped the other writers develop the model. It is used across the board to prove or disprove specific theories. Below are some examples of how Occam's razor has been used in the past.

> **Religion-** The model has been used to attempt to prove or disprove the existence of God.
>
> **Scientific theories-** Scientists use the model to decide whether a hypothesis is genuinely purposeful. If it is

easy to be proven or falsified, this is usually a good start. The more complex the hypothesis is, the denser the facts have to become to justify the theory.

Medicine- Doctors use Occam's razor every time they see a patient. They attempt to find the fewest causes for multiple symptoms and the most likely cause of their ailment.

As with any model, always keep in mind that they are not 100 hundred percent fool-proof. That is why it is a process - a discovery through facts and theories - to find the correct answer. Always draw the conclusions you believe will fit best with the situation, and never be afraid to discredit the model if it doesn't fit in with the project at hand.

Every problem that you solve is an opportunity to better your critical thinking skills. Rather than looking at problems that may arise as challenges that are impossible to meet, use this step-by-step system to break down the elements of even the most complex issue and find a method of approaching it. In time, you will see that not only your thinking skills, but your problem-solving skills will have developed.

What You Will Need to Succeed

Don't worry. You won't need a dictionary or thesaurus to wade through this book. But you may want to make some notes.

Writing down key ideas and figuring out what they mean to you just happens to be a critical thinking skill. So, even as you learn about critical thinking, you'll be doing it!

If you wanted to become a better swimmer, you would read up on how to do it better but eventually, you'd have to wade on into the deep end. That's kind of how we'll handle this material. We'll explain how it works, show you how it's done, and then let you try it for yourself.

So, pick up a plain composition notebook or any kind of lined writing tablet and something to write with, and let's get started and head for the critical-thinking, decision-making pool, no beach towel required.

Chapter 1
What is Critical Thinking and Problem Solving?

Problem solving is that term that has found its place in most fields. However, each of these fields has a different perspective on what problem-solving exactly is. For example, in psychology problem solving would be defined as finding a solution to any mental issues or processes where as in statistics it would be defined as a method to obtaining a solution for a certain issue on how many fish are there in a lake.

One must remember that the problems can also be categorized. These categories would be well-defined problems and ill-defined problems. Ill-defined problems, as the name suggests are problems that do not have a clear cut goal. It makes it difficult to come up with solutions to such problems. You might not be able to identify an expected solution. Well defined problems, on the other hand, are those problems to which solutions can be found easily. These problems have well-defined goals which make it easier to estimate the magnitude of the problem and also identify feasible solutions to the same. We might also be able to plan in advance if we identify such a problem.

When you are faced with a problem in any field, or even in your life, you might either try to solve the problem through logic or by trying to interpret the problem. No matter which method you use, you have to first understand the goal of the problem and also try to identify the different routes you can take to solve the problem. This is the key to problem solving! You might sometimes have to resort to abstract thinking and try coming up with a creative solution.

For instance, consider that you teach a bunch of 10 year olds English. You have to cover the different parts of speech in an hour's time. You know that the children that you teach have a low attention span. Your problem here is to grab the attention of the kids for an hour in order to help them understand the parts of speech. You could either go about teaching them in the regular manner by using the text or you can make it fun for them! This is a problem where you would use abstract thinking in order to find a creative solution. You know that your children love games. So you can come up with a brilliant game that they will enjoy. But ensure that this game also teaches them the parts of speech!

Critical thinking is a learned skill and it can benefit those who become adapt at using it in every decision they make. As a critical thinker, one of your goals is to become more familiar with your subconscious mind and to learn about the mechanics of the knowledge base that resides there.

Critical thinkers know that arguments are created in such a way for people to have ways of determining the validity of everything that happens in the world. In most situations, you may not even know whether you were able to make the perfect argument in proving that a claim is valid or not. However, the way you argue would be the one that would count.

Types of Critical Thinking

Logical Reasoning

In its formal sense, logic is a system of rules according to which one may make inferences or draw conclusions. In other words, logic dictates how facts and conditions can be used to gain new understanding.

For example, if we begin with the factual statement that "A beagle is a type of dog," and then add the fact that "Rover is a beagle," we can then conclude that "Rover is a dog." However, if we are told "Scruffy is a dog," the laws of logic do not allow us to conclude that "Scruffy is a beagle." All beagles are dogs, but it does not follow that any dog is a beagle, so we cannot say anything else about Scruffy.

Notice that the logical example above does not show evidence for any of its claims. The facts we started with (a.k.a. "premises") are true for the sake of argument. This is why critical thinking requires evidence as well as logic, to ensure that logical claims reflect reality.

Scientific Reasoning

The scientific method is the process by which scientists and many other scholars and critical thinkers use tests and experimentation to support a claim. It is a general mode of thinking that—while primarily associated with experiments in the physical sciences such as biology, chemistry, and physics—is also prevalent in the social sciences as well as in philosophy and other disciplines.

The scientific method begins with a specific question, such as "How can I use electricity to power something?" or "Why are people suffering from this disease?" The person wishing to answer their question then provides a "hypothesis," an educated guess that they believe is possible based on what they know already. They will then conduct a test in the form of several experiments or the collection of data relevant to the problem. They may experiment with different models for harnessing electricity, compare the health records and routines of the patients living in the infected region, or simply try different brands of detergent. They then analyze their findings to draw a conclusion.

Experiments are often replicated to test results under different conditions. For example, if the experimenter found a correlation between people suffering from the same diseases in a certain area and their ingestion of a chemical in the water, they might conduct an experiment on lab animals using those chemicals, or find another population demonstrating a similar correlation and analyze them.

The Psychology of Critical Thinking

Critical thinking in psychology is defined as the habits and skills to engage in activity or exercise with reflection and criticism focusing on deciding what to believe and decisions to make. Critical thinking is a tool that is important even in psychology, and it is being taught in psychology classes. Many students coming to college have already formed theories and opinions of the subject and of life in general. When they are faced with college work, they get a shock when they find it is not what they thought it would be. Some students opt to cram the textbooks so that they will help them in the exams forgetting learning entails more than that.

Four Goals for Critical Thinking

An adept critical thinker learns that the process requires a commitment to four goals each time it is used in order to get the most out of the endeavour.

Self-Direction

The first goal will be to strive for self-direction. Self-directed learning involves taking responsibility for your own acquisition and analysis of factual information from which you will learn. Your decision to dig deeper into ideas requires you to step out of your comfort zone, and you are going to have to make a decision about whether becoming a critical thinker is worth it to you. It is much easier to take things at face value – advertisers, marketers, politicians, and many others prefer that you not become a critical thinker, in fact! Most people are quite comfortable following cues from their highly conditioned subconscious mind and going about their days living in a world where they roll right along with the status quo and, quite frankly, lead mediocre lives.

Self-Discipline

The second goal as a critical thinker is do develop a strong sense of self-discipline. Learning and practicing critical thought is very challenging. Becoming a practicing critical thinker does not happen overnight and must be looked at as a process that takes a lot of introspection, self-analysis, and a commitment to change. And, if you have ever decided to learn a new skill and found it very difficult in the past, it is quite possible that you thought about giving up at some point because you found the work too hard. This is why so many New Year's resolutions are broken every year. As an example, one can visit a fitness centre on January 2nd of any given year and usually find it to be very crowded, and visit the same fitness centre forty-five days later and see a marked difference in attendance. Self-discipline is not easy.

Self-Monitoring

The third goal for a critical thinker is self-monitoring. The biases and stereotypes we have taken on in our lives are a direct result of our past experiences and the knowledge we have acquired from those experiences, as well as from what we have learned from those around us, and they may or not be accurate to some degree. Your mission as a critical thinker is to question your preconceived notions about your world and to assess and evaluate their level of accuracy as you move forward with your new ways of thought.

Self-Correction

The fourth goal a critical thinker must strive for is one of self-correction. This occurs when we reflect upon how we have perceived things in the past and then make decisions about the accuracy of those perceptions. This can be especially difficult because the knowledge base that resides in our subconscious has been hard-wired over the years. In order to have the self-discipline to correct erroneous thinking patterns (see how these goals work together?), we have to see the value of doing so. Critical thinkers will undoubtedly tell you that the benefit is that when you seek out and study various perspectives of issues, there is an opportunity for personal growth. They will also tell you, though, that questioning and correcting inaccurate perceptions that have been held throughout your life may cost you in terms of relationships. Not everyone around you will understand why you are suddenly questioning beliefs that they have held along with you for so long.

How Do You Identify Whether or Not You Are a Good Critical Thinker?

Critical thinking is a trait valued by many employers, and it is likely that they will test your critical thinking skills during the interview process. However, if this trait was not tested for, your work will show how good of a thinker you are. A weak critical thinker will begin to make costly errors. These mistakes will be repeated, which shows a lack of learning and a weak thinker will be unable to determine where action is necessary. These people will make assumptions, and the majority of their assumptions will be incorrect. This list continues to grow as better ways to evaluate a critical thinker are developed.

First, there has to be a question. It doesn't have to be impossible to answer, but it should be more complex than "What colour is that car?" or "Where did you get your shirt?". Often, good questions include a political issue, but you would also use critical thinking to determine where your next move should be or what you should major in.

Second, you have to examine the evidence. This won't involve pulling fingerprints or examining blood splatter samples, but you want to look at the big picture. Take on that omniscient point of view.

Third, analyze any assumptions or biases. How does that work? Say you are talking to your friend about how her boyfriend treated her. She is upset; therefore, you can assume that she may not necessarily lay any fault in herself or she may exaggerate the situation. It's important to comfort your friend, but from a critical thinker's standpoint, you would want to consider this bias or even get the story from the boyfriend's point of view.

Fourth, remove your emotions from the situation. Like in the previous example, your friend is unable to properly evaluate the situation because she is upset and emotionally involved. This is why it is smart to go to other people for advice about big decisions. Emotions clutter and often take over the mind because, of course, we are all only human.

Fifth, when you think critically, you want to consider other interpretations. So let's talk about things from the boyfriend's point of view. Maybe what offended your friend was not intended by her boyfriend, and thus miscommunication caused the argument. This is something you should consider when trying to seriously guide your friend through this difficult time.

Sixth, sometimes, even after considering all of the information you possibly can, there are still some questions left unanswered – that's okay! Though you would like to know everything, sometimes every bit of information is hard to find. This is known as ambiguity, and to think critically, you don't need to eliminate it, but you do need to consider it.

Sometimes, what you do not know is important when it comes to decision-making. When thinking critically, you must determine the ambiguity to determine whether you even have enough information to make a clear, rational decision about a topic.

Helping Your Child Think Critically

It is easier to learn things when you are younger because many habits have not yet been formed. When you are an adult learning how to think critically, you have already spent so long thinking more simplistically that you will really have to try to think critically. For children, even toddlers, this will be a beneficial skill to learn.

You can add critical thinking to playtime. For example, when they get a new toy, instead of showing them how everything works and where the buttons that make it light up are, give them time to figure it out. At first, they will probably throw it or bang it on the floor or even take a taste test. This is okay – it is their way of learning. Once they are done with their initial evaluations, either they will give up on it and go play with a toy they know how to use, or they'll continue to investigate.

If they keep investigating, that is awesome. Their little gears are turning up there! If not, give them a nudge, give the toy back to them and ask suggestive, open-ended questions like "What is that?" or "What does this one do?". It is likely that they will respond positively to your questions. If you are excited about this new toy, they'll be excited about the new toy.

If you have asked all of the questions and given them a little more time and they are still not all the way there, now you can give them a nudge in the right direction. Now you are going to ask questions that will help them hypothesize – obviously they won't know these complex terms, but the learning process is still the same. Ask them things like "If we touch this, what will happen?". This could prompt them to press buttons or turn knobs.

You can also encourage them to think critically by talking about what you are doing. If you're playing with a light-up toy, say "Let's press the button" before you press the button. Verbalizing your thought process can trigger their thought process in the same way.

It will be a very rewarding moment when your child is happy because they figured it out on their own. Their successes will make them more confident and motivated to find out how the next toy works.

Fighting Biases

Recognizing your viewpoint is as important as recognizing the viewpoints of others. This allows you to understand and limit biases. First, you should understand how to find these varying points of view. Talking to people is also useful; politics is a difficult topic to discuss, and a lot of people shy away from it when it's brought up. But if you truly want to eliminate bias, you should at least do your research.

We all know that interaction over the Internet is a million times easier than face-to-face interaction. This is detrimental in some ways, but it makes learning easier. Doing research is another way to identify different viewpoints. Bias is very apparent in everyday life, whether it is directed toward big-picture things, such as the daily roles of men and women, or affording certain licenses toward people because they are famous or attractive. To think critically, you must recognize the presence of bias and eliminate it.

Being biased can be a sign that you are too close-minded or one-sided. To eliminate bias, you must practice what was outlined above. You can see that many of the things on the path to critical thinking are intertwined. Being open-minded and fair were two of the characteristics of a good critical thinker. These things will also help control and eliminate biases in a situation. A lot of the time, bias can be eliminated by removing yourself from a situation or understanding the other side's point of view. That being said, you don't necessarily have to be opinion-less in this situation. You want to make an educated decision about which side of an argument you choose to eliminate bias. By being educated, you are not being one-sided because you evaluated all positions being taken which is open-mindedness.

Biases That Directly Affect Critical Thinking

There are different levels of consciousness; therefore, there can be different levels of bias. Recognizing how this affects our ability to think critically is important.

These are four common biases that can be taken out of the picture once you are aware of them:

> **Action bias**: think before you act! Critical thinking flies right out the window when you act before properly evaluating a situation.
>
> **Confirmation bias:** you are not always going to be right. Lots of times, you will want to take the path that will confirm what you already know. Don't – humans

aren't perfect! You are not always going to be right! So while you are looking for evidence that supports your viewpoint, don't disregard the information that discredits your viewpoint. Often at times in a debate, the opposing viewpoint should be acknowledged to strengthen your argument anyway.

Association bias: this can be avoided by identifying correlation versus causation. This ties into a lot of superstitious beliefs – not washing your uniform before a game and believing something bad happened on Friday the 13th because it is a day of bad luck are a couple of examples. Recognizing the difference between a coincidence and two things that are actually related will help eliminate association biases.

Chapter 2
Build Your Problem Solving Skills

Problem Solving Skills

When it comes to problem-solving, critical thinking is crucial because when solving problems, you need to apply logic and reasoning to whatever situation you will be facing to find suitable solutions to problems. Critical thinking will enable you to view situations from different angles. Let us look at the different qualities of a problem solver so you can know what you can do

Qualities of An Efficient Problem Solver

To become an efficient problem solver, you will need to be:

Be Open-Minded

Do not go into a situation with the aim of being the 'hero' or 'saviour'. This will only serve to cloud your judgment because you will take it upon yourself to provide all the solutions. A critical thinker knows that his way or his approach is not the only one, and it may not be the best; hence, the importance of being open-minded. When you are open-minded, you will listen to others and seek solutions that will work best, even when the solutions are not something you provided.

Empathetic

To improve your problem solving skills, you must look outside yourself. Empathy allows you to do this; it removes internal focus from your biases, and shifts it towards someone else. When this happens, you begin to see situations through the eyes of someone else as it were. If you are empathetic, you will also improve your communication skills, your people skills (cooperation with other people), and your ability to work with others.

Employ Rational Considerations

Problem solving should not use emotions, faulty, or incomplete information as its basis. Instead, it should use rational considerations as its base. This means that you need to find out what is truly going on, and gather all information before you make any judgments. Your solutions should use facts and evidence as its base. Your own opinion and emotions should not incapacitate your judgment.

Problem solving simply entails finding solutions to different situations, problems, and challenges you face. It is an extremely crucial skill to build and improve because effective problem solving is what helps you combat challenges, ease your struggles, and find innovative fixes to the most bizarre and seemingly unfixable problems.

In addition, problem solving is a lifesaver when it comes to making decisions. If your problem-solving skills are good, you are likely to make a well thought-out and fool proof decision quickly and easily.

Nobody has great problem-solving skills at birth; we learn these skills and build them over time.

Here are some sure-fire ways to do that.

#1: **Become solution focused**

When facing a problem, most of us panic and fixate on the issue at hand. Neuroscientists have discovered that your brain is incapable of finding any solutions when you fixate on the problem.

Focusing too much on the problem narrows your ability to see possibilities because you keep reminding yourself of how hard the problem is and feeding your mind negative ideas. This triggers undesirable emotions that block your ability to come up with good solutions.

To become a good problem solver, shift your focus from the problem onto the solution. Well, you need not rule out the problem entirely. You just need to treat it differently and train yourself to pay more attention to identifying a way out of the quandary.

- When stuck in a rut, first acknowledge you are stuck. Saying things like "I am stuck in this problem" or simply observing your emotions and allowing your fear, stress, and sadness to subside on their own helps too.

- Once the emotions have settled a little, focus on the situation at hand and analyze it non-judgmentally and closely.

- Every time a negative thought pops into your head, replace it with a positive suggestion and say things like "I am finding solutions for my problem" to yourself repeatedly.

- Think of ways to fix the issue and write them down.

- When finding solutions, list down as many as you think of, even the ones you find ridiculous or impossible at first.

- Keep your mind open to whatever you can think of to improve your creativity.

- Once you have listed down a handful of solutions, analyze them in detail weighing the pros and cons of all options against one another.

- Choose a solution with the maximum number of pros and least cons and implement it immediately.

When you start focusing more on the solution, you think with optimism, something that broadens your horizons and helps you come with innovative and effective solutions to all your challenges.

#2: Clearly define your problem

Oftentimes, the solution hides within the problem, and the only way to figure that out is by clearly defining the issue. When we face a problem, we just perceive it from one, narrow-angle; we rarely dig into its root cause.

To define it clearly, you need to focus more on the 'why' part of the problem.

The example below shows you how to do it:

If your problem is that you are always late for work, you need to ask yourself the following whys and answer them accordingly:

- "Why am I always late for work?" "Because I keep snoozing my alarm so I can sleep more."

- "Why do I feel like sleeping more?" "Because I feel really tired when I wake up."

- "Why do I feel exhausted even though I've just woken up?" "Because I sleep late daily."

- "Why do I always sleep late?" "Because I keep surfing the web or binge watching shows on Netflix late into the night."

- "Why do I engage in the activities highlighted above?" "Because I feel bored."

- "Why do I feel bored?" "Because I don't have good friends or healthy activities to engage in to feel entertained."

Use this strategy to dig into all your problems until you have a clear picture of the underlying issues, causes, conflicts, etc. Once you dig that out, you resolve it first and slowly resolve all the whys you listed out earlier.

Following the example used above, you can start by building a habit of playing tennis with a friend an hour before your bedtime so you feel entertained and exhausted and go to bed on time to wake up fresh the next day and get to work on time.

The next time you face a problem, use the process illustrated above to define it clearly so that you can figure out the correct way to resolve the issue for good.

#3: Make things simpler

When we experience a challenge or difficulty, we normally fret because we tend to overcomplicate things. Things are usually not as complex as we make them out to be. To fix your issues, simplify things as much as possible. If you feel worried and unsure of snagging the promotion you have been eyeing for months, do not concern yourself with who may get it; focus more on improving your performance to increase your chances of attaining it.

Break down a problem to it's simplest form and you will easily find a solution.

#4: Think laterally and work on your inner-language

Again, when most of us experience a challenge, we tend to focus on just one side of things. This is a big reason why we never come up with out-of-the-box solutions.

Turn things around by thinking laterally so you change your flow of thoughts. Try to look at things from a new angle by flipping your objective around. To come up with a new solution, go outside for a stroll and get some fresh air, take a few deep breaths and keep asking yourself "How can I do things differently?" Or "What would someone smarter than me do in this situation?" Doing this will make you think of alternate solutions and broaden your way of thinking.

Additionally, work on using a 'possibility of creating language' in your routine talk. Every time you face a problem, think in terms of "What if I do this?" "How about I try this technique out?" "What other techniques might other people use?"

This encourages you to think positively and create possibilities in your head so you can come up with great, innovative solutions. At the same time, avoid using negative and closed statements such as "This is not possible" "This will never work."

Such statements limit your possibilities and ruin any momentum you have on solving the problem.

When you implement these tactics, observe how they work out for you and improve on the mistakes you make so that you achieve better results on the next try.

The Benefits of Problem Solving Skills

Critical thinking is the one aspect you are going to use most in your life if you want to take your life from something that is just plain and simple, to the next level. Every person on this planet has problems.

These problems come to us in a variety of ways, and they are different for each one of us, but the point is, every single one of us has problems. Now, many of us sit back, close our eyes, and hope that our problems will go away on their own.

But they don't.

In order to solve your problems, you are going to have to think about them in a critical manner. Pick those problems apart. Look for solutions. Look for ways you can use aspects of the problem to your own advantage.

Think about the problem personally, and independently. Advice from others is great, but at the end of the day, it is still *your* problem, and *you* are the one that is left to deal with it while it is there and ultimately solve it.

The Danger of the 'Fix It and Forget It' Method to Problem Solving

Society today is both blessed and tarnished with the information that is available on the Internet. We all go through our days, and when we need something that we don't know, we consult the Internet, fix the problem, and move on.

There is almost a robotic movement that is going on here, and it is one that doesn't aid in the realm of critical thinking. We glance through the solution on the Internet, then we close our computer and go on with our day… there is no lesson learned, and nothing that can be applied to another situation.

Of course, a lot of people argue that there is nothing wrong with this. That we will always have the Internet with us, and there is no need to worry about actually learning the method because we will always be able to just look it up.

To an extent, they are right about the access to the Internet being something that is relatively constant for many of us, but they are wrong in the aspect that we need to develop the skills needed to solve problems.

You are faced with decisions all day long, and without the necessary skills to solve them, how are you going to progress in life?

For example: You can look up on the Internet how to make a cake. How to drive a car. Even how to build a car. When it comes to things like that, you are set.

But you can't ask the Internet if you should apply for that job that is in the next town. Or if you should invest in your friend's business idea. Or how you are going to apologize to your wife when you feel that you are the one in the right.

These are real-life problems, and they are things that Google will never know the answer to, even if you were to ask a thousand times. This is why you need to develop your own problem-solving skills, which is largely sourced in critical thinking.

Don't Just Look at a Problem or Decision You Have to Fix. Analyze It.

When you are faced with a decision, whether it is a problem that you need to fix or a decision that will better your life, you need to ask yourself what *you* would do. All too often, when things like these arise, we run to our friends and family to ask them what they would do in that situation.

The problem with this is that what is best for someone else may not be what is best for you. You may opt-out of a great job opportunity because your cousin said they wouldn't do it. Or maybe you let your marriage fall apart because your buddy wouldn't try to fix it if he was in your shoes.

Don't get me wrong, advice is always a great thing to have, but you can't base your actions or your life on what other people would do, you have to ask yourself what you would do, and what you should do.

Weigh the pros and cons to any situation. Ask yourself if it would work out better one way or the other. Ask yourself what the risks are, and if you are ok with losing whatever the risk may be if you lose the gamble.

Life is a series of questions and decisions that you need to learn to make, and one that you need to learn to live with the consequences. Critical thinking is a great skill to have, it is going to help you learn how to develop these other areas in your life, and ensure that you are happy with the results.

That is the entire point of analytical thinking when it comes to problem solving and decision making. When you ask everyone else what they would do, you are avoiding taking responsibility for the outcome. If it works out great, you are happy, if it doesn't, then you can blame the other person for not making a decision that worked out great for you.

If you develop your independent thinking skills, then you can make your decisions in full confidence that they are going to turn out great. Of course, there is always the risk that something could go wrong, but at the end of the day, you know that you were able to make the decision knowing what you were going in to on the outset.

It is a very different way of dealing with your problems than if you are always asking someone else what they would do. You will learn to stand on your own two feet on any issue, and you will find that you are able to make decisions with confidence.

Improving Decision-Making and Problem-Solving Skills

The worst thing that tarnishes our ability to make decisions is that we struggle because we are afraid of making the right one. In fact, the majority of the stress that we feel comes from being afraid that we might not be making the right one. Decision making isn't an easy process. This is why we often have others make the decision for us! Think of the last time that you went to the grocery store. Maybe you weren't sure what snack to buy. A display of candy bars or chips that were on sale helped make your decision. Then you got home and plopped in front of the TV, ready to find something good to watch. Rather than scrolling through, you went with the first pick of what was recommended for you. It felt like you made a decision, but most of these choices were made for you throughout the day.

When we struggle to make decisions, we struggle to problem solve as well. If you aren't sure of yourself, don't think critically, and have mental fog, then it will be hard to make a quick decision. Not all problems need instant solutions, but many of us still struggle to come up with the right answer because of all the other thoughts jumbled within our brain. In this chapter, we are going to give you the best decision-making and problem-solving methods so that you can think as fast as possible without letting these processes slow you down.

Making decisions can be hard because there's so much other fluff that can get in the way of clear thinking. Imagine that you are trying to make a cake in your kitchen. If stuff is cooking in the oven, there are dishes in the sink, and another person is trying to make a meal as well, it will be harder to focus on the cake! We have to keep a clear head in order to make it easier to think quickly. There are a few steps to do this:

- Prioritize your thoughts.
- Look at the most basic version of the problem or decision.
- Conduct an analysis to find all possible options.

Let's first take a look at the how-to of prioritizing the most important thoughts.

How to Prioritize Important Thoughts

To work optimally and get the things done that need to be taken care of, you'll want to learn how to better prioritize the things that are most important to you. We often try and do the things that we want to get out of the way at that moment. Maybe you're cleaning your home and you have to do the dishes, do the laundry, and clean up your room. As you walk throughout the house, however, you see smaller tasks that need to get done, so it's easier to get distracted. What's most important, however, is that we prioritize the things that we initially wanted to get done as they are essential. You didn't think of completing the other tasks until they were right in front of you. So is it really all that important to you?

Sometimes everything seems like it is important. Your brain can be very good at convincing you of certain levels of urgency. Anything could be meaningless or dire if you thought about it.

If you have a problem or need to make a decision, there are some prioritization tools that you need. First, write a master list of everything needed to know about this situation. What needs to be done? What are the problems that are going to keep you from completing these tasks?

First, decide the level of importance, how quickly it needs to be done, and the estimated time that it will take to complete. Sometimes you will discover a problem that can be easily taken care of when you are able to prioritize properly.

It is essential that you narrow your options to the very core. You won't be able to make the right decision if you aren't properly prioritizing your thoughts and actions.

Sometimes we struggle to make a decision because we are scared of what will happen if we don't make the right decision. We don't think about what that worst-case scenario is even going to be! Next, make sure to remind yourself to look at the past and discover that things turned out completely fine. You are OK today, so even when you made the wrong decision, everything ended up working out.

After this, use examples to help you make decisions. If you're really stuck, Google your specific question because someone online has likely had the same dilemma. Yahoo Answers, Reddit, and Quora are great user-based tools that many people use to share their struggles online. You can get multiple answers if you ever need more advice than what you are already experiencing.

The best decisions will be made when things are planned out, and you can't do this if you aren't properly planning in the first place! Sometimes we have to make sure that we plan before, rather than waiting until after we face the problem, to make the right decision.

How to Identify the Real Issue

One method for problem solving is to look at the real issue that needs to be confronted. We often try to find solutions that will help get us out of a situation fast. You might want the quick fix or an easy alternative so that less effort is required. However, if you do try to take shortcuts, it can end up hindering your ability to find a positive solution in the end.

Sometimes, the person making the decision doesn't want to have to admit that they're wrong. Maybe it's a spouse, a boss, or someone else that refuses to accept responsibility for the outcome. What can you do to help get to the root of the issue? How can you find a solution without having to make them feel bad or prove them wrong in the first place?

It is important to train your brain to go directly to the core. Always ask "Why?" Go through the normal questions of who, what, where, when and why. Dig deeper and use your critical thinking skills to get you to the real problem that's hidden underneath it all. Think of the last time you had two friends fighting. They might have fought over something small, maybe one was rude to the other, or perhaps there was a little misunderstanding. Between two average individuals, maybe it's not a big deal, but these friends might have blown things out of proportion. Part of this is because there was likely a deeper issue hidden underneath the rest that made everything feel worse than what it was.

To understand how to make the best decisions and come up with the greatest solutions for certain problems, you can use a root-cause analysis. There are a few steps to this process. As an example, we are going to use the idea of someone that struggled to lose weight because the diets they have tried never worked.

First, identify what the issue is at face value. What is the most basic understanding of the problem? In our example, it is that someone struggles to lose weight.

Share this problem with someone else. Discuss it and gain a different perspective. In this example, the person that wants to lose weight might talk to a doctor, nutritionist, or even someone else that shares their struggles.

Look at all the things that could have caused or influenced this issue. This is when thinking becomes deeper. In this example, they struggle because they suffer from anxiety. Their mother was very hard on them about losing weight. They use food as a source of comfort. Exercising is difficult for them.

Come up with a few different solutions. At this point, you can see the many different causes; therefore, you can develop different solutions. In this example, you might talk to a professional about overcoming anxiety so the emotional eating stops, and they can work through issues with their mother. A better exercise routine can be presented as well.

Choose the solution that will work best. This would be dependent on the individual, but as you can see, the solutions that we came up with aren't simply "find a new diet plan" because that is not going to solve the root of the problem.

Decide if this was the right thing to do. After this analysis has happened and a solution is chosen, it's time to implement the strategy. The person trying to lose weight can see a therapist and sign up for a yoga class.

Fix and prepare anything else needed for this process. This is when you would reflect and determine if the best course of action had been taken. If weight loss is occurring, then the right solution was found. If no weight loss is happening, it's time to dig deeper or try out a new solution.

How to Use Reasoning, Judgment, Analysis, and Learning

Sometimes we want to find a solution to make the situation in front of us. When we do this, we can quickly forget that there are alternatives available to us! Remember to start with reasoning. Don't look at things from your perspective. Consider all avenues of equal importance.

Next, you can form judgments. These judgments should be objective, but they can also be from your perspective. There are a few ways that you can improve your judgment skills. Make sure to recognize the faults of your past in order to pull valuable information that will keep you from repeating mistakes. You also have to recognize the biases that you experience. These include things such as:

- Your level of optimism/pessimism
- How much you favour a person/place/idea

- Your expectancy of an event based on the probability that it has happened in the past
- The ability to notice details/larger concepts

Make an analysis. Were you right / were you wrong? What needs adjusting? Here are your how-to steps of proper analysis:

- Break it down into pieces to start with one area at a time.
- Create a goal for what information you'd like to pull.
- Gather all the important information needed.
- Make judgments and correct the process to gain desired results.

Finally, you will take away something that you learned from this experience. Even in the most challenging scenarios, there will be something valuable that you can pull.

To increase your ability to do all of these things, you will have to research, practice, research, practice, and repeat over and over again. Practice is something that you have to do on your own

Chapter 3
A Portrait of the Critical and Not-So-Critical Thinkers

Strong critical thinkers are more effective in life. They are able to approach situations in ways that make more sense and are able to be defended logically. They are less prone to being caught into behaving in ways that are impulsive or incorrect, and because of that, it is imperative that you learn to be a critical thinker. The critical thinker is going to find that getting through life is simply easier—it is everywhere in life. The ability to think critically is necessary in so many situations around you, from how likely you are to succeed in a job that is quite technical and mathematical to how likely it is that you will be able to have a happy and successful relationship. Let's stop and take a look at some of the most notable traits of both a critical and not-so-critical individual to see the real difference between the two.

The Critical Thinker's Portrait

When you develop your ability to think critically, you see a boost in all sorts of characteristics that can make you more desirable socially. You will become someone that more people want to be around, and more emotionally intelligent—one of those buzzwords in today's society that means that you get along with people better and are better able to manage your relationships and interactions with other people thanks to your ability to understand and control yourself and your own emotional states. This is all due to a culmination of several other traits, such as:

Inquisitive

The critical thinker is inquisitive—they are constantly willing to ask questions and understand the world around them. They are driven by their desire to understand others better and will make it a point to learn about several different issues in the world in order to have a clear understanding of how they impact others.

Attentive to Times Where Critical Thinking Is Necessary

The critical thinker is well aware of the strength of his or her abilities and is constantly on the lookout for situations in which critical thinking is necessary and warranted. Whenever it feels like critical thinking could be relevant, it is used, even if it seems like there may be an easier, simpler solution.

Self-Confidence

Because the critical thinker is aware of his or her abilities, there is confidence developed. The critical thinker is confident that he or she is able to reason and trusts that it will be done when it is necessary.

Open-Mindedness

The critical thinker is willing to recognize that world viewpoints are different, and that is okay—they are willing to entertain other opinions and assertions, giving them the same benefit of the doubt that they would give to others.

Flexibility

The critical thinker is aware of the fact that flexibility is needed sometimes, especially when considering opposing viewpoints or viewpoints that do not align with their own personal beliefs in the first place. They are willing to think about those difficult issues with the attention they deserve and will not shut down when presented with a viewpoint that does not align with their current one, and they are able to roll with the flow when something goes wrong and needs to be changed accordingly.

Alertness

The critical thinker is well aware of what is likely to happen in the future in order to begin anticipating anything that may happen as a result. These people are usually closely watching politics and political tension in order to figure out what to expect around them.

Understanding Other People's Opinions

The critical thinker is likely to listen to what other people think, even if they disagree with those beliefs, or they feel like they are irrelevant or unimportant. They will make it a point to listen and understand the other person's opinion rather than immediately dismiss it as illegitimate.

Fair in Appraising Reasoning

The critical thinker will not unfairly judge other people's approaches to their own reasoning—they will make it a point to give every argument a fair judgment. An argument will not be dismissed for not aligning with the critical thinker's own personal opinions.

Honest

The critical thinker is able to understand his or her own biases and prejudices, and in being honest about those biases and prejudices, he or she is able to correct for them, so they do not become problematic in the first place. This is an ability to self-control and self-regulate.

Understanding When to Stop, Make, and Alter Judgments

The critical thinker is able to understand when it is appropriate to stop attempting to make a judgment, to make one, or to change one, based on feedback and understandings of the situation.

Willingness to Reconsider and Revisit Viewpoints When Change Is Necessary

The critical thinker is able to recognize when it is important to reconsider what he or she was thinking about a situation in order to alter a viewpoint if it has since come to light that the viewpoint made was something negative or not able to be validated in some way, shape, or form.

The Not-So-Critical Thinker's Portrait

The not-so-critical thinker is someone unable to manage thinking critically on a regular basis. This can result in someone who is largely considered biased or judgmental, such as someone who is unwilling or able to accept the judgment that someone else is passing on them or someone who simply sees no reason to think critically about a situation. These people may struggle in their relationships and careers, as it is much harder to find a job that will literally never require some sort of higher-level thinking skills. Nevertheless, let's stop and look at some common characteristics of the not-so-critical thinkers.

Pretentious and Unable to Accurately Self-Analyze

Someone struggling to think critically is likely to be quite pretentious—they may say that they know or understand out of embarrassment rather than admit the truth, and they are frequently unaware of their own weaknesses or limitations.

Think of Conflict as a Threat to the Ego or an Annoyance

Someone struggling to think critically is likely to see any sort of conflict that may arise as a threat to the ego rather than something that requires attention. If anyone tries to refute them, they are likely to feel threatened or annoyed and dismiss the claims without reflection.

Impatient and Unwilling to Spend the Time to Learn

Someone struggling to think critically is likely to constantly be impatient—if something is complex, they will skip to the end with a best guess rather than attempting to really understand it. They would rather rush through to the end instead of learning, even though this means that they are still left in confusion.

Follow Gut Reactions Instead of Evidence

The not-so-critical thinker is likely to focus on feelings and gut reactions. When they are asked if they want to get the sports car or the SUV, they are going to opt for the sports car because it makes them excited, even though they could really probably find better use with the SUV. They are so caught up in their feelings that they do not pay attention to data and evidence, and this can cause them to behave impulsively instead of logically.

Preoccupied with Themselves

To the uncritical thinker, they are constantly correct. They are preoccupied with their own opinions of the world, and because of that, they are unwilling to entertain anyone else's viewpoint. As soon as someone voices that they disagree, the uncritical thinker starts focusing on how best to refute the claim rather than making it a point to learn the other person's viewpoint, which may be quite valid. The preference will always be given to viewpoints that are in agreement with them or in viewpoints that are supportive of their own.

Chapter 4
Critical thinking: skills and competencies

Many people have difficulty in logical and consistent reasoning. But it is very important to understand that reasoning skills, like any others, can and should be developed in oneself. Initially, for this, it is worthwhile to understand what critical thinking is in general, and begin to apply its techniques in practice.

Critical thinking is a whole complex of fundamental skills, such as the ability to give assessments, make conclusions, interpret and analyze, observe, etc. In addition, critical thinking uses logic and is based on a series of criteria of intelligence: clarity, credibility, accuracy, depth, significance, horizons and justice. The constituent parts, albeit to a lesser extent, are also value attitudes and creative imagination.

Speaking a little differently and simply, critical thinking can be characterized as cognitive activity associated with the use of reason and intellectual abilities. When a person thinks critically, evaluates and analyzes the data obtained, he uses attention, categorization, choice, judgment and other similar mental operations. The application of critical thinking makes a person a number of requirements.

Considering critical thinking as a process of reflection, we can see that it requires a person to have a considerable amount of skills. These include:

• Ability to determine the position of another person, his arguments and conclusions.

• Ability to evaluate evidence of an alternative position.

• Ability to impartially and objectively evaluate opposing arguments and testimonies.

• Ability to identify false opposites, see pitfalls, read between the lines.

• Ability to recognize the techniques used to give a particular position more attractive than others, for example, all kinds of methods of persuasion or false logic.

• Ability to think in an organized way and complement the process of thinking with logic and insight.

• Ability to determine the validity and validity of conclusions, guided by reasonable assumptions and solid evidence.

• Ability to summarize information and combine judgments of evidence to form their own opinions.

• Ability to present one's point of view in a reasonable, organized and convincing way.

In 1987, one of the best American educators, Robert Ennis, also managed to identify the abilities and attitudes associated with critical thinking. They are:

• Scepticism about things.

• Ability to reason.

Talking about the development of critical thinking will be incomplete if we do not mention scepticism. From the point of view of critical thinking, scepticism assumes that a person casts some doubt absolutely everything that he encounters. This does not mean that he does not believe everything he hears or sees - he simply acknowledges the fact that his views can change if he receives any additional information.

Critical thinking suggests applying doubts and scepticism constructively, evaluating all available information. Thanks to this, we can make more informed and objective judgments on what we consider productive, correct, true, and vice versa. It also significantly increases the effectiveness of our decisions.

There are people who seem more trusting than others, and there are those who are more sceptical. The reason lies both in personal qualities and in the life experience of a person. But critical thinking is neither an innate feature nor a character trait - it is a specific method that allows interpreting events in a certain way. Sceptics can take an orderly approach, and gullible people can simply question everything constructively.

As for the reasoning, here we are talking more about rational thinking. Rationality involves the use of reasons to explain phenomena, events, and facts. And reasoning, as a rule, always starts precisely from oneself. It looks something like this:

• Initially, a person finds reasons: why he believes in something or does something (at the same time, he realizes what these reasons are)

• He then critically evaluates his actions and beliefs.

• In the end, he can explain the reasons for his actions and beliefs to others.

At first glance, all this is very simple, because it seems to us that we know why and what exactly we believe. But in some cases, doubts begin to overwhelm us, as a result of which our own beliefs no longer seem so true. In fact, we really have no idea about the completeness of the information we possess and we begin to think: maybe everything that we hear or see is just one of the variations?

There are also cases when we are not sure whether we are explaining something correctly and acting correctly. Therefore, it is necessary to resort to the development of observation and study the basis of your own reasoning, beliefs and actions, because only they will help us conduct any critical analysis.

But we must not forget that critical thinking is basically a critical analysis of the reasoning of others. To conduct it, we must not only be able to find the main argument of another person but also be able to analyze and evaluate its details.

Any reasoning, either one's own or another's, consists of an analysis of the evidence and conclusions drawn from it. Evidence supports the findings. For example, you think that it's cold outside today. You tell someone about this, but he does not agree with you, and wonders why you got this. As proof, you can cite what temperature the thermometer shows and your own observations of the weather outside. In this case, your evidence will be ice on the ground and a low-level temperature outside.

And when we critically analyze the judgments of other people, we can and should conduct the following mental operations:

- Define reasoning and conclusions based on them.

- Analyze how the interlocutor chose, combined and ordered judgments orderly (this way we will determine the course of reasoning).

- Evaluate the extent to which reasoning supports findings.

- Assess the validity and evidence of reasoning.

- Identify inaccuracies in the reasoning process.

We apply reasoning similar to the example of the weather, which we use literally hourly in everyday life. But when we study or work, we need slightly different considerations with a formal structure (for example, reports and essays) and for the formation of such reasoning, additional skills are required, namely:

- Skill in the selection and structuring of reasoning (needed to confirm the conclusion).

- The skill of consistent reasoning.

- The skill of applying logical order.

- Skill of effective use of speech means (needed to represent the process of reasoning).

Everyone, who is interested in the development of critical thinking, should pay special attention to the development of three basic competencies, on which all the others are based. Among these competencies:

• Ability to think. Critical thinking is the ability to organize, categorize, select, differentiate, compare and contrast.

• Emotion control. Critical thinking is an impartial process, but emotions can prevail at any time. This is normal, because often you have to make a choice between different positions and points of view. Sometimes they can unsettle evidence that is unacceptable to us, or unexpected arguments. In most cases, emotional instability only worsens the situation, and the ability to control one's emotional state is a useful and effective skill, as it allows you to calmly bring logical arguments and convince the interlocutor.

• Research and knowledge. Even knowing how to think critically, it is not always possible to find good and convincing evidence without understanding the subject. Critical thinking is also a skill in conducting your own research. Remember that the ability to find data on any issue will make your life easier, because you will be able to capture important information and provide alternative evidence, evidence and explanations.

Critical thinking, among other things, requires a person to have accuracy and accuracy, as well as an irrepressible desire to find the right answer. So, what we have:

• Be objective; be able to give up their personal preferences, beliefs and interests during the conversation in order to better understand the topic and come to a more accurate result.

• View the subject from different angles, i.e. explore information from different perspectives.

• Repeat, i.e. discuss the same issue several times in order to take into account the maximum number of details.

• Be mindful of details, i.e. develop observability and devote time to finding even the smallest details that could lead to clarification of the issue as a whole.

• Identify trends and patterns, i.e. analyze, organize information and identify repetitions and similarities.

• Consider distant prospects and possible outcomes, i.e. keep in mind that what appears to be true may now be called into question after a while.

Chapter 5
Logical Thinking: Facts and Logic

The simplest explanation of critical thinking is that it is your thoughts plus truth. If you take nothing else away from this book, the importance of facts and logic cannot be stressed enough. The most crucial thing you can do to develop as a critical thinker is to support what you think, say, and do with facts, and subject it to logical scrutiny.

As stated earlier, critical thinking is the ability to analyze facts in order to reach a conclusion logically. A fact is a statement that can be supported by external evidence or observable experience. Facts are certain, and they are true. Elementary, you say? Maybe the definition is simple but applying it has been the subject of philosophers and scientists for centuries. We'll talk more about facts later, but for now let's just say that it is something that we know to be true, whether it is because we observed a certain action, scientists tested a physical principle in a lab, historians have used rigorous methods to ascertain its existence, etc. Facts are the bricks that make up critical thought.

Logic is the mortar binding the facts together. Logic is simply the set of rules and relationships governing claims about the truth and falsity of statements. In plain English, logic lets us determine when we can say two different statements lead to a new statement. The classic example in freshman philosophy classes is "All men are mortal. Socrates is a man. Therefore, Socrates is a mortal man." It sounds basic both since all of us have already internalized some level of logical thinking, and because this common sense statement disguises an abstract law of logic. In this argument, the premises, or the starting points established as true for the sake of discussion, do allow us to make a new statement. We also know that we cannot say "All mortals are men" because our experience shows that there are mortals who are not men.

In this case, logic doesn't allow us to make the statement "All mortals are men." It does not follow from the premises, and it creates an invalid relationship according to other rules of logic. Logic prevents us from making contradictory statements, from saying things that simply do not make literal sense.

A defendant's alibi is a simple example of logic preventing invalid conclusions. If we know that the accused was in a different place during the actual crime, we dismiss the case because we also know that a person cannot be in two places at the same time. It's also why we tend to be suspicious of politicians who make contradictory claims—you can either want to do something when you're in the office or not want to do it. Saying two different things is not only confusing when it comes to predicting the candidate's policies, but it is also logically invalid.

Logic lets us gather facts into new insights, rather than letting facts simply exist like so many pieces of a broken puzzle. Conversely, facts make logic have real consequences, rather than simply remaining abstract figures on paper. Facts and logic are the foundation for critical thinking, so get into the habit of identifying the facts and logic behind the statements and attitudes around you, including your own. You may find considerable gaps in this area, allowing you to question things and present new ideas, or you might be able to reinforce those statements with facts and logic. The point is that in critical thinking, supporting our statements is as important as making them in the first place, and there are specific ways we should be supporting those statements.

Intellectual Rigor

Just like there are certain standards that determine if food is safe or a ball has been thrown out of bounds, critical thinking asserts that there are standards when it comes to how we justify our thoughts and claims.

US Senator Daniel Moynihan once famously stated that "Everyone is entitled to his own opinion, but not his own facts." This is a classic statement of critical thinking. We'll talk more about facts later, but for now let's just say that a fact is a statement that has "truth value," meaning it can either be true or false. An opinion is a subjective matter. We may feel strongly about it, but it is not true or false in any sense beyond the opinion holder's mind or heart. When we assert something as factual, we are inherently making a claim about its truth-value and why we are asserting it is true or false. Confusing fact and opinion is a symptom of muddled thinking, and critical thinking tries to remove that confusion.

How we arrive at the particular truth-value of a certain statement should conform to standards of clear thinking, evidence, and rationality. Let's say somebody made the statement "All red-haired people are stupid." You could take that statement at face value, but that wouldn't be an example of critical thinking on your part. You could try to interview every single redhead around the world, but even if you could do that, you'd likely soon meet an intelligent redhead that disproved the speaker's statement. So, how might that person justify that statement? They might say they have met a lot of redheads and found them to be stupid. Yet again, a lot of redheads are not the same thing as all red-heads. Also, how did this person establish their stupidity? Do they have an intelligence test? Was that test designed by people with valid measures of intelligence? There was likely no such test. Like all statements of prejudice against a group, this statement will eventually have to fall back on a subjective value judgment that has no truth value—for example, an opinion being used to support a false statement.

The intellectual rigor of critical thinking can often seem harsh or insulting. After all, anytime those standards are asserted, there will be varying levels of different people meeting or falling short of those standards. "How could you vote for that person?" is a well-known inquiry that can expose a lack of critical thinking on the voter's part and even a sense of smugness from the one asking the question. Voters don't always vote rationally, according to the facts, or even according to their own self-interest in the long term. They often rely on first impressions, catchy slogans, and rhetoric, or the opinions of those around them. Critical thinking may not always put the best person in the office, but it will be the best method to make that determination. Awareness of flawed thinking is painful, but it is necessary if we care about critical thought informing important choices.

Intellectual rigor can seem like the most daunting aspect of critical thinking, but it is also most rewarding. It takes effort, concentration, time, and probably some reading and studying when we're especially hard-pressed for an explanation. Yet we are also challenging those around us, and ourselves, to rise to a higher standard.

Seeking Straight Answers

Another large part of critical thinking is the ability to explain why you are doing something with a careful, reasoned explanation (rather than simply saying "Because I felt like it" or "Someone told me to do it"). While this may sound rather lofty, at the same time your explanation should be clear and orderly. It should reflect a clear line of thought, traceable back to factual premises, and it sticks to the facts as well as the topic at hand. Irrelevant information, ideas that don't flow, or off-topic tangents are another sign of a poor argument.

Have you ever encountered someone who replied to a question without actually answering it? Did they get off-topic or immediately shift to a whole new topic? Critical thinking ensures you stay on-point. Steering the person back to the question not only demonstrates a sharp mind but simply gets you an answer to your question.

Did the person answer your question with a lot of jargon—for example, technical terms only known by experts, with vague terms or cliché or without a clear beginning or end to their answer? In other words, did they provide deliberately sloppy or confusing answers? Ask them to make their answer clearer, sticking to simple terms. Critical thinking is not (always) a matter of complex language, fancy terms, or long-winded responses. Clarity of thought and communication is a hallmark of critical thinking.

Thinking About Your Thoughts

Without sounding too abstract, critical thinking involves thinking about our thinking. In plain English, it means paying attention to how we derive judgment. It entails holding our decisions to a higher standard.

The simple act of asking ourselves "why" we do certain things or even have certain opinions or attitudes is a huge part of critical thinking. Many organizations have powerful mission statements, which outline the organization's purpose and philosophy so that management and staff alike can always remind themselves why they work there in the first place. On the ground level, projects often get off-track because the project goals are no longer the focus. Sometimes simply asking Why certain things are being done again can help people focus back on the goals.

The "Why" question can often lead to "how," generating broad questions that can actually lead to specific understanding. "How did I come to believe in the things I now believe?" may sound like an unnecessarily abstract--and possibly intimidating--question, but it could also lead to a better understanding of ourselves and our values. Instead of answering, "That's just what I believe," you begin to have concrete, articulate explanations for your beliefs.

Above all, critical thinking concerns itself with the method—with how we arrive at a judgment. It's why a scientific experiment operates according to accepted practices based upon scientific data: so that the experimenter can say that his results are based upon an established method, not mere conjecture or sloppy design that might have thrown off the results. It's also why we have standards when it comes to things like construction or food safety. The method leading up to the result must itself be sound, or we cannot rely on that result.

In your own life, simply asking "What was my chain of thought leading up to this decision or judgment?" is a crucial act of critical thought. You may discover you didn't have all of the information needed when you made a choice—or that some of your attitudes are more the result of a particular upbringing and hearing the same ideas.

Rather than being something passive we do between action, thought becomes an active guide to those actions, something we are aware of and can therefore subject to scrutiny, in order to improve it.

You're the One in Charge

Critical thinking is the discipline of taking full responsibility for your thoughts and deeds. You are the one who arrives at a conclusion based upon evidence examined by you, actual experiences you've had, and logically approaching the world around you. Your beliefs are your own, rather than ideas forced upon you by habit, circumstance, threats, or other external factors. You are taking charge of the ideas and stimuli around you and subjecting them to examination. You may incorporate other people's ideas, but only when the ideas themselves have been vetted--not because the person giving you those ideas claims to know more, not even if everyone else tells you that they know more.

There is any number of political debates about a slew of topics going on at any time in this country. Just flip on the television or check a social media website, and you can hear someone citing statistics to back up their side in the debate. Next time that happens, try conducting your own research. Check where the speaker may have found their data. Did the speaker leave anything out? If you can find the source, look into whether that source has any political or economic interest in a particular political outcome for that issue. Then find out if another source has a different set of statistics or even a different interpretation of those numbers. Contrary to popular belief, even though "numbers don't lie," they can be conveniently abbreviated or interpreted to suit one side's needs.

You may find two different interpretations of the statistics, or even two completely different statistics. You may then need to determine which of the two is more reliable according to a neutral source, or if anyone is actually presenting the whole picture. The point of this exercise isn't for you to establish rock-bottom certainty on an issue (though if you can, good for you). The purpose is to familiarize yourself with not accepting everything at face value, with questioning claims around you and with using your own mind to find out more and draw your own conclusions. That is critical thinking in a nutshell.

The German philosopher Immanuel Kant famously advised people "Dare to know!" This perhaps odd little phrase carries with it a rather subtle definition of "knowing." For Kant, his fellow Enlightenment thinkers, and critical thinkers throughout history, "knowing" is a deeply personal, self-determined act. Kant was reacting against a culture built around following a certain authority without question. At a time when more voices than ever claim authority, his advice is timely as ever.

Brainstorming for Critical Thinking

This is the method where people use brains to storm or examine a problem. Its aim is to develop many ideas in the shortest possible time to solve an identified problem. The generated ideas eventually help to find the best solution possible for a given problem.

How Is Brainstorming Applied

Brainstorming is a tool applied in many institutions so as to generate as many ideas as possible in a team. The focus is usually on the number of ideas brought up but not the quality of the ideas. The groups are usually made up of 5 to 15 people with attention put into the composition of the group. A consideration is made to ensure there is a variety of experience, knowledge, and backgrounds in order to produce varied ideas from varied perspectives.

Brainstorming is usually applied at the beginning of a project when there is no clear definition of the project possibilities. This is a useful way of coming up with ideas that are creative in production methods or product development. Marketing and advertising objects are popular for brainstorming. Brainstorming helps stimulate a group's creativity and encourages the bringing up of unconventional ideas. Every contribution is welcome and may lead to a diversity of ideas.

It is imperative for there to be a clearly defined question before brainstorming starts. However, it is important to note that brainstorming is not as effective on problems that are complex or difficult to describe or those that require specialized knowledge.

Rules of Brainstorming

The most important rule is 'postponement of judgment.' Criticism or feedback is not allowed during the brainstorming session. Every idea is welcome whether common or uncommon, obvious to absurd, impossible to clever ideas. Brainstorming is about gathering as many ideas as possible when criticism is introduced, it blocks free thinking and discourages contribution of ideas instead of motivating each other to generate more ideas. In a brainstorming session, every person must feel free and safe to contribute. The rules in brainstorming are to allow space and remove any obstacles to allow free thinking. Some of these rules are:

1. Postpone judgment – every idea is good, acceptable and noted down, criticism waits for later

2. Focus on quantity – the aim is to gather as many ideas as possible

3. Freewheel – there is freedom to jump from one idea to the next and even to think aloud

4. Hitchhike – it is allowed to hitchhike on another idea and apply synergy and complementing each other by continuing to work on the idea

The Process of Brainstorming

Brainstorming usually takes place in a session, where participants gather together to stimulate and motivate each other to come up with many ideas. The session begins with a well-defined and stated problem. This enables everyone to be able to focus on ideas that are aimed at answering the question or solving the problem. In a brainstorm session, there is usually the team leader who directs the discussion. There are various phases of brainstorming. These are:

- *Preparation*

The sessions comprise of about 5 to 15 laymen and experts. The group is informed beforehand the problem or question to be discussed, date, time and duration of the brainstorming session. All the materials needed are prepared by the team leader prior to the session.

- *Generate Ideas*

All ideas that are generated are noted down on a flip chart or sticky notes or even recorded by the team leader. The team leader ensures every person participates and gives their ideas and creates a relaxed and creative atmosphere. This first phase of generating ideas is called the divergence phase because of the diverse ideas generated. The next phase is the convergence phase where the different ideas are grouped together into related subjects.

- *Evaluation*

After the brainstorming session is over, an evaluation of all ideas is done. This part can be done using the same participants or narrowing the group further down. Evaluate the usefulness of the ideas on each topic of discussion, analyze their pros and cons and compare the ideas to each other. Prioritizing takes place, and the hanging fruits or ideas that offer immediate possible solutions are given first priority. When you filter the best and most useful ideas, you begin to move from quantity to quality.

- *Creativity*

Brainstorming is much more than just presenting ideas, but it is a way of developing more creative ideas in a short time. Every person is creative and is cable of advancing their creative skills. There are several ways to stimulate creativity according to psychology—hence helping you to have better critical thinking skills. These methods include:

- Remember ideas – always ensure you have a pen and paper. Ideas come at any time, and the best way is to note them down immediately to enable you to remember them later by referring to them.

- Challenge yourself – try to do something outside your comfort zone to stimulate new ideas. A new challenge stimulates the brain to get creative solutions that may also have a positive effect in other areas.

- Widen knowledge and skills – applying knowledge and skills to new situations is called creativity. Learn new skills by attending seminars, reading or watching documentaries. Stay open to learning new things—hence stimulating your brain to be more creative in thinking.

- Stimuli – creativity is promoted in an environment with stimuli like music. Stimuli provide impulses for the brain to be more creative in thinking.

Chapter 6
Making Better Decisions

In this chapter, you will learn about the distinct decision-making styles that people have. It would be unwise to assume that your decisions only have a personal impact. There are certain decisions you make that will affect the lives of others, so it's important to understand your style of making decisions. If you are a leader in some way or intend to lead people in the future, you need to read this chapter.

There are four general styles of personal decision-making. These are Directive, Analytic, Conceptual, and Behavioural. You should know that nobody fits entirely in one single category. It is likely that you have traits that cut across two styles.

On the other hand, there are also group decision-making styles. These relate to how you tend to lead a group of people when making a decision. These are also divided into four categories. These are autocratic, democratic, collective, and consensus style. Each of these affects a group in a different way and can be effective in unique situations. If you are in business, you need to understand these styles.

So, which of these decision-making styles best describes you?

Personal Decision-Making Styles

Directive Style

If your decision-making style is directive, it means you value structure above all else. You are aggressive and expect instant results whenever you give an order. When you encounter a problematic situation, you take charge, make fast decisions, and expect everybody else to do as their told without asking any questions.

As a directive decision-maker, you have learned to depend entirely on your own experience, knowledge, judgment, and information. You are a stickler for the rules and have excellent verbal skills that allow you to give clear directions.

However, there are some limitations to this style of making decisions. You tend to act very quickly without waiting for all the facts. This means that you are likely to make rash decisions without assessing other alternatives. It is also possible that your decisions provide short-term benefits but no long-term solutions.

Analytic Style

If this is your style of making decisions, then you are a born problem-solver. You just love examining all kinds of problems, challenges, and puzzles and figuring them out. You are innovative and enjoy dealing with large quantities of data every time you are required to make a decision. Clearly, analysis-paralysis means nothing to you. No matter how challenging the problem is, you are adaptable enough to handle it all.

On the flip side, however, you are also a slow decision-maker. The fact that you tend to wait for all the data and facts to come in before making a move means your decision-making process can be very time-consuming. To some extent, some people may describe you as a control freak.

Conceptual Style

As a conceptual decision-maker, you see problems from an artistic perspective. You tend to be very creative when solving problems. In fact, you try as much as possible to come up with solutions that are fresh and new. Unlike a directive decision-maker, you believe that every solution must be long-term. You try to think about how your current decisions will impact the future. As a result, you are a risk-taker and extremely achievement-oriented.

Behavioural Style

You are a natural peace-maker who believes that every decision must bring people together and avoid conflict. You are very diplomatic and excel at persuading people to see your point of view. Since you are a people-person, you prefer to work in a group so that everyone agrees on the best action to take. This gives you the opportunity to help people reconcile their differences and agree on one acceptable solution.

Group Decision-Making Styles

Autocratic Style

This is a decision-making style where you, as the leader of a group, take total control of every decision. You don't even bother to ask your group members for their opinion or ideas on how to solve the problem. You simply decide what to do depending on your own perception and internal information. As a result, you are held completely responsible for both the positive and negative results of your decision.

The autocratic style of decision-making is very effective when the group needs to make a quick decision, for example, during an emergency. However, this style also brings a lot of challenges within the group.

Group members may not be enthusiastic about implementing a decision that was made without their input. For example, if the decision affects employees negatively, morale will go down and they will become resentful toward the manager. Therefore, productivity within the company will be affected and the manager may no longer be seen as being a credible leader.

Democratic Style

This particular style allows you to make quick decisions by involving the entire group. As the leader, you give up your control and ownership of decision-making and allow group members to vote. The decision that gets the majority of the vote will be adopted and implemented by everyone.

The problem with this style is that, unlike the autocratic style, there is no sense of individual responsibility. No single member can be held responsible for any decision the group makes, and if something goes wrong, one member may refuse to accept responsibility because they voted against the decision in the first place.

Collective Style

This is where as the leader of a group, you get everyone's input about the situation and involve the members in every step of the process. However, the final decision rests with you alone. You encourage your group members to share their ideas and any information they may have about the situation. As they do this, you gain greater insight and a wide range of perspectives on how the problem may be solved. At the end of the day, you analyze the input you have received and make your decision.

In the collective style of group decision-making, you have to accept full responsibility for the outcome of your decision. The advantage of this style is that everyone gets the chance to be involved and participate in the process. For you to succeed as the leader, you must develop excellent communication skills and become a good listener. This is the best way for you to get a clear picture of the situation so that you make the best decision possible. On the other hand, the fact that you have to wait for group input makes the decision-making process very slow.

Consensus Style

This is quite similar to the democratic style, but what makes them different is that in the consensus style of decision-making, the decision must be unanimous. As a leader, you have no control over the final decision and do not have to accept individual responsibility for the outcome. Everyone must agree, otherwise, the decision cannot be regarded as consensual.

The biggest benefit of this style is that it creates a strong sense of commitment within the group. Everyone feels like their opinion matters and plays a part in the success of the group. By involving every single member of the group, you will increase the likelihood of achieving success. The consensual style of decision-making is usually used when you have a small group of people who will be working together for an extended period of time. A good example of this is a business partnership.

The only downside is that the decision-making process will be slow. It is also difficult to teach a group of people to work together like this and still maintain harmony.

How Seasoned Executives Make Decisions

A manager is paid to make decisions. This is what executives do all day long. However, if you examine the way managers at different corporate levels make decisions, you will notice an interesting trend. Research shows that managers at different levels have different decision-making styles. Furthermore, a successful manager changes their decision-making style over the course of their career. As they get promoted to more senior management positions, the way they critically analyze business processes also evolves.

When you are at the lower levels of a company, your primary responsibility is to ensure that products get out the door and any hitches are immediately resolved the moment they arise. In other words, taking action is everything. When you move higher up the ladder, your job isn't about taking action. Now you will have to decide which products or services deserve to be created and the best method to develop them. In other words, if you intend to become an effective manager as you ascend the corporate ladder, you must learn how to change how you utilize information and analyze options.

However, there is one warning you need to heed. If an ambitious lower level manager tries to adopt the decision-making style of an upper-level executive too quickly, they will set themselves up for failure. Likewise, if a recently promoted upper-level manager gets stuck with the decision-making style of a lower level executive, they will ruin their career. The key here is to ensure a gradual and seamless transition pattern.

But how does this transition occur?

Research shows that a successful low-level supervisor uses a decision-making style that is the total opposite of a successful CEO. As a manager rises up the ranks, there seems to be a gradual progression toward a more participative approach with a greater diversity of opinion. However, the supervisor who spends most of his time on the shop floor needs to be more direct and command-oriented. They don't have time to listen to everyone's input because quick action is demanded of them.

This narrative makes sense because when a manager is at the top of the hierarchy, they lose touch with what is happening on the ground. Therefore, their decision-making style must be geared toward gaining as much information from multiple sources as possible. For a senior executive to be successful, they must encourage people to give them information so that they can critically analyze all the data and select the best strategy. In fact, the most successful business executives become more flexible, open, and analytical in their decision-making style as they climb up the corporate ladder.

But at what point does this shift occur?

There appears to be a "convergence zone" early in the managerial hierarchy, right between the manager and director stage. At this level, an executive will discover that the decision-making style that was effective in the past no longer works. Therefore, most managers simply try to achieve a balance by adopting new styles while still retaining much of the old ways of thinking.

But this is where things get interesting. Most successful managers are able to let go of their previous decision-making styles and adjust to new styles. This rapid evolution is what propels them forward in their careers. However, unsuccessful managers seem to get stuck in this convergence zone for too long. They notice that their decision-making style isn't working, but for some reason, they don't know how to deal with the situation. So they try to use a variety of styles at the same time. They try to be direct today and participative tomorrow. They are action-oriented yet also try to be open to other options. Instead of allowing their decision style to evolve and progress up the ladder, they hold on to former ways of doing things. Unfortunately, it is in this zone that the least successful 20 percent of managers fall and stagnate for the rest of their professional careers.

Why You Need to Know Yourself

When you finally get to understand how you make your own personal decisions, you will be able to adjust your style to suit the situation you are facing. This will impact the kind of results you get. You need to know how to look at a problem, pick the most appropriate decision-making style, and then use it to develop the best solution possible. Whether you are a student, an employee, or a CEO, you can benefit from learning how to manage yourself and others.

In the business world, it is vital that you learn how a shift in corporate hierarchy affects your decision-making style. You do not want to get stuck doing things the same way as you did in the past. There are many talented managers who have crashed and burned simply because they failed to critically analyze their corporate transition. The bottom line is that you need to recognize the best time to evolve your style and just do it. Don't get stuck in the convergence zone.

Problem Solving Best Practices

From the spat you broke up between your children earlier in the morning, to the project that is looming over your head at work, we use our problem-solving skills on a regular basis. This world is made up of an array of different people and it is not crazy to think that we would all need to have some basic problem-solving skills. Children learn these skills when they are just toddlers, advancing forward on two feet, exploring the world around them without holding mommy or daddy's hand. We naturally develop problem-solving skills, though some aren't as strong as others. In order to grow better at this tool, there are several best practices you can follow.

Systems

I know you've probably heard the word systems about nine hundred times, especially if you work in a traditional corporate career, but there is definitely a reason for that. As problem solving, decision making, bright-eyed employees, it's vital to have control over our ability to be creative, but creative doesn't mean chaos. A systematic approach that is in line with your workplace or home conditions and constraints will really assist you in moving forward in the process.

Let's face it, stressing out over problems is already hard enough but to add chaos to the mix is asking for trouble. Maintain a structured environment and approach to your job and you will find it helps with organization and focus as well. No matter the situation, find a system to complement it. Systems are the key to an organized, functional work and home spaces. It's already crazy enough out there in this world, don't make it any harder on yourself.

Turn That Frown Upside Down

When a problem does come up, stop what you are doing for a moment and remember that with every problem comes a lesson. Instead of getting irritated and frustrated with the problems, view them as opportunities for a better and more knowledgeable self. Oftentimes you will find that problems become life-changing events, especially when it comes to the brain and how you perceive the world around you. Make the most of every situation, no matter how hard it may seem.

Perspective

Perspective can be the difference between stress and anger and an understanding of others views and sides. Changing your perspective on things allows you to see a little bit better into the world around you. There is always a multitude of ways to solve a problem, but if you feel like nothing else is working, begin to change your own mindset. You may also want to seek advice or time with a psychologist to discuss the other troubles you have.

Sometimes taking a break from the situation can help tremendously. Being overrun is not fun, and adds trying to cook, take care of the kids, and take care of your significant other. Oftentimes, that small hour break brought me back to my current place in life with a renewed and refreshed ability to handle any problem sent my way. All it took was a change in my own perspective.

Evaluation

While I understand that we, as part of this society, receive more than enough evaluations through our lives, this is about you evaluating yourself. Let's face it, we aren't always master at our own success. We go through the motions, finding ourselves bottlenecked in a situation or issue. When this happens, it continues to pull and tug at our irritation and lack of focus. Sometimes stepping back and re-evaluating our processes can help to unlock that kink in our creative nature.

Even in the times you aren't struggling with a cramped brain or a brick wall, evaluating and starting fresh on a regular basis is an amazing way to bring vitality back into your personal and professional life. Evaluations don't have to be professional, but you have to have a thorough idea in your head what conditions you work best in. That way when you are changing your processes, you change them for the better.

Chapter 7
Use of Critical Thinking to Tackle Challenges

It is possible you have seen the standpoint of cognitive psychologists regarding the relationship between the act of thinking and the sense of feeling. These experts defy common belief that the first thing you do when something happens is to feel or show emotions, and only after that do you begin to ponder over what happened. Cognitive psychologists do not agree that feelings come automatically, and, as such, precede all other senses. On the contrary, they hold the premise that the feelings you carry result from your own thought process, and so if you can influence your thought process, you also can change the way you feel. Essentially what is being said here is that if you think of a good outcome, you will be happy even before you have seen the results, and if you think of a bad outcome you will feel low and lose motivation even before you have begun your process.

The Emotional Power of Human Beings

You also have the power to do the following:

- Influence your feelings by controlling your thought process, and this, of course, is one way of embracing critical thinking

- Influence your attitude, so that by the end of the day you have a positive world outlook. With a positive attitude, you can make judgment without prejudice, and give room for critical thinking.

- Influence your thought process so that you are able to direct your actions accordingly, and you get your anticipated results. Practically speaking, engaging in critical thinking keeps you away from stress, because at every juncture you feel you are in control of what is happening. In fact, you can fall into depression by the mere feeling that you have lost control of what is happening in your life.

- Effectively, therefore, critical thinking is not just great for success, but it is also great for your welfare.

The question that then begs to be answered is if there is actually room for you to ever behave or act instantaneously. And the answer is in the affirmative. It is very normal, as a human being, to develop feelings, even when you have not given much thought as to how you are about to feel. Nonetheless, after studying the benefits of critical thinking, you would be expected to halt and say, "I know what feelings influence my thought process negatively and which ones have a positive influence. And so I'm choosing to influence my thought process in a way that will be fruitful, rather than allowing my feelings to run amok."

Once you are informed the way you are after reading this book, you are able to quickly dissuade yourself from acting out of raw emotions. What you often find yourself doing, and which brings harmony and success to your life, is moderating your emotions, and this you do by actively engaging in critical thinking.

Can you now say you know something worthwhile about critical thinking? All right ... however, there is a simple assessment you can do, to see if you have truly mastered the necessary skills to make you successfully undertake critical thinking.

How to Test Your Mastery of Critical Thinking Skills

Whenever you are skilled at critical thinking:

- You rely on reasoning more than you do on emotions
- You do not stubbornly stick to your viewpoint, but rather you accept that it's better to evaluate different points of view
- You listen to what other people have to say, all this with an open mind
- You are prepared to receive fresh evidence whenever you are evaluating an issue, and you are also glad to accept fresh findings as well as new explanations,

irrespective of whether the phase being discussed is deeply underway and is probably nearing completion.

- You are open to reassessing the information you already have
- You are prepared to set aside personal prejudices, and also ignore any biases you ordinarily have
- You are perceptive to vary options
- You are able to avoid the temptation to hastily make conclusions, and just as hastily make judgments

Looking at these points, you may conclude that critical thinking comes easy to you, but just believe it, there are many people who do not think critically when faced with a problem that needs to be solved. As such, it is important to learn the easiest way to learn critical thinking, and also the most convenient steps to take in employing those skills.

How to Carry Out Critical Thinking Step By Step

Establish What the Problem is

Why is it important for you to see what the problem is from the start? If you consider that you can employ resources addressing an issue only to discover you are following the wrong trail, you can see what a waste of resources that can be. Other times, if you do not first try to identify the problem, you end up spending a lot of your time and other resources, only to establish there was no problem in the first place, probably just a situation misread.

Undertake to Analyze the Problem

Why spend time analyzing the problem you have already identified? Simple – you want to know the exact nature of the problem, the areas of your project it is affecting, its magnitude and even your capacity to handle it. It is at this stage of analysis that you determine if the problem at hand is one you can deal with as an individual, if you require some additional assistance, if it is one a problem that can be handled instantly or if it can only be tackled at a later stage in the process, and such other matters of a fundamental nature.

Think up Manageable Solutions

Yes, you do not just delve into solving a problem without knowing the chances your chosen method has of working. Since you are, presumably, a serious thinker, and not an amateur trying to solve a problem on a trial and error basis, you need to weigh the options you think may work in your particular situation, and then pick the best. As someone who is looking for the best output for your project, you need not shy away from consulting, if it comes to it, as it is usually helpful to have different perspectives on the problem. Brainstorming is also very helpful.

Choose the Best Possible Solution

Even though there are many roads that lead to Rome, so to speak, it would be reasonable to choose the one that is the most cost effective and the one that has the least inconvenience – and then you would term it the best. Here, too, is a case where you are likely to have several possible solutions to a challenge, and you cannot, obviously, use all of them. So it is up to you to weigh what advantages each of them has over the others and how convenient the one with the most advantages is to apply – and then you can term it your best possible solution. Remember as you pick your best option it is necessary to take into account the prevailing circumstances.

Wind Up Your Process

How else do you wind up your process but by implementing your best solution? You cannot possibly go on searching and comparing notes, and marvelling at the wide range of choices that you have, like some people go to school and study this, and then proceed to study that and the other, and hardly get to the point of putting to use what they have learned. Remember the starting point of this process was identifying the existing problem, and you, therefore, made it your goal to look for its solution. Now you must, of necessity, take the relevant action, to see to it that the problematic issue you pointed out has been resolved.

So, if someone were to anticipate results, would you say they should wait for a drastic change in the issue at hand? To be safe, you need to say, not necessarily. Guess what? Sometimes doctors diagnose your medical problem and, after due consideration, decide you are better off living as you are than putting you through medication, surgery or any other medical procedure. Likewise, there are some issues that are best left as they are, because any changes to them would adversely affect more people than is the case in the prevailing situation.

In short, critical thinking can give you justification to change matters, and it can also make you see that the situation as it is remains the best possible scenario. However, even when you choose to let the issue or situation remain unaltered, you need to say as much in writing, and then state the reasons that prompted you to arrive at that conclusion. When you make your stance and reasons known, everyone concerned finds it relatively easy to accept your verdict, and to live with the situation.

Do you think solving a particular problem is the only achievement you get after engaging in critical thinking? Gladly, it is not. For starters, all the information you learn from the process of critical thinking cannot be ignored. It is wealth that you can fall back on in the future if you are faced with a similar challenge. At the same time, you come from the task with a fresh boost of confidence, mainly emanating from the fact that you understand the issue at hand from all possible perspectives. So whatever the project is about, there is no fear that something untoward can crop up and take you by surprise.

Finally, the more informed you are and the more you have practically analyzed and tested scenarios, the more resourceful you become, even to people around you. And even if there was no challenge in the foreseeable future, who says there is harm in keeping your skills sharpened and your wits about you?

Extrinsic and Intrinsic Motivation

Think about what motivates you to do the things you need to do every day. Salespeople are often motivated to go out there in the world and sell their wares because the more they sell, the more money they will make. Children are motivated to clean their bedrooms because if they fail to keep their rooms clean, they may receive some sort of punishment from their parents. People who routinely drive fifteen or twenty miles per hour over the speed limit will often slow down and follow the speed limit when their radar detectors begin to beep, fearing that they may get a speeding ticket if they fail to do so.

The above examples are all illustrative of what is called **extrinsic motivation**, which is motivation that is coming from sources external to the person being motivated. The behaviour in which they are engaging may not be something they would typically do unless there was something or someone external to them that is pushing them to something or not to do something.

Intrinsic motivation, on the other hand, is motivation that comes from within. Consider a woman who decides to begin a running exercise routine not because anyone tells her to, but simply because she enjoyed running as a younger woman and wants to feel the joy of being out on the track again. Another example is the young man released from prison who, even though he has external motivators like probation or parole that will help keep him in line, is motivated from within to get a job and to stay away from the behaviours that led him to jail because he truly wants to make a better life from himself. A third example is a man and a woman who decide to enrol in a critical thinking course or read a critical thinking book together because they believe that learning critical thinking skills will help them improve their relationship.

Which type of motivation do you think has a more significant impact on lasting behaviours? Studies show that the stronger motivators come from within, and that makes sense because if one has internal reasons for wanting to engage in certain behaviours, chances are that they can revert to that reasoning for support when their motivation wanes.

The trick, though, is to continually tap into that internal motivational reasoning for reinforcement, especially when defence mechanisms or faulty thinking are vying for attention in the mind. This is why you need to practice critical thinking, or anything else you are motivated toward doing or not doing, on a routine and regular basis. Internal motivation is also bolstered by positively affirming commitment to the task and by reading about your goals on a daily basis.

And although motivational forces that live external to you are not as powerful as internal motivational factors, it does not hurt to garner support from other critical thinkers or other people involved in the process of learning the tenets of critical thought. As we have said many times throughout this book, the process of learning and practicing critical thinking can be challenging and lonely sometimes and the more internal and external motivation you have, the stronger you will be as you persevere on your journey toward becoming a practicing critical thinker.

Chapter 8
Win An Argument Every Time

By utilizing critical thinking and understanding the 25 cognitive biases, you will be able to form an argument. However, there is more involved in arguing. There is also more that can affect your argument, aside from the 25 cognitive biases. To do this, you must first understand what an argument is made of in order to form an argument of your own.

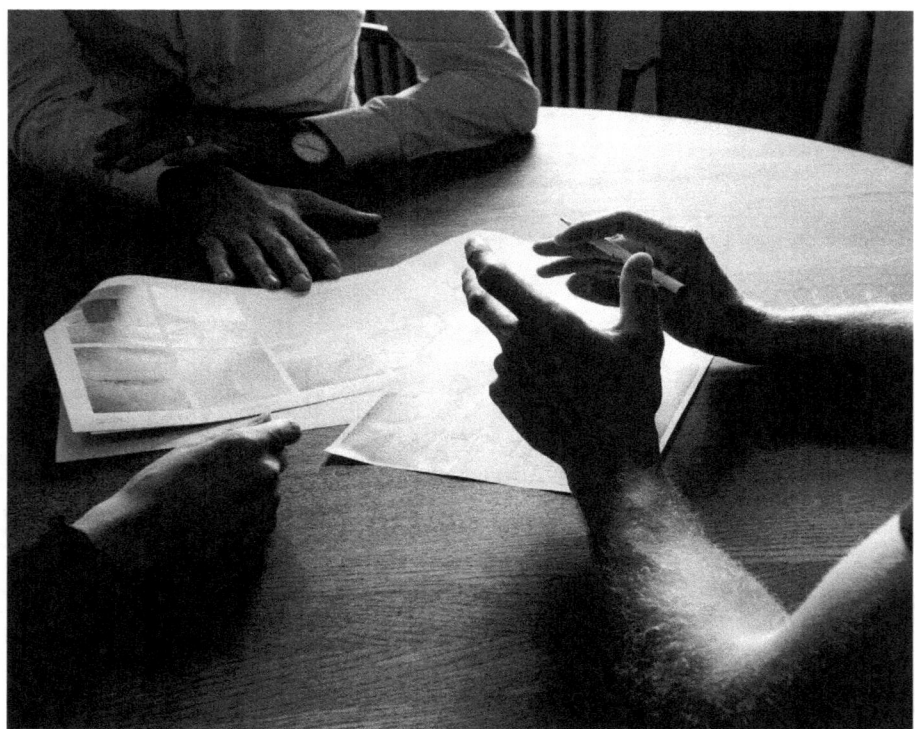

If you look way back to ancient times, the logic of Aristotle remains true even though thousands of years have passed. His argument consisted of two main parts: the premise and the conclusion. A premise is going to support the claim that is being made. Think of this as the supporting details. The conclusion is going to be the claim that is being made. However, to get to the conclusion, your premise must be logical and lead to the conclusion. When creating an effective argument, you want your reasoning to be sound – don't leave anything out. Make sure that the premise or premises support the argument. When all of your premise/s support the argument, the argument becomes valid. You also cannot twist the truth in any of your premises if you are looking to create a sound argument.

Let's look at a valid argument and an invalid argument. Each of these will have two premises and one conclusion. An argument can have several premises and a single conclusion and still be valid. In fact, the more supportive premises you have, the more sound your argument will become.

All men are mortal. This is a premise. It is a fact rather than an opinion.

Socrates is a man. This is another premise. It is also a fact, and the conclusion will help link the two premises to each other.

This means Socrates is mortal.

The next example is an invalid argument.

Socrates is mortal. True, this is the conclusion that we came to in the previous argument. What goes wrong is in the next premise.

All men are mortal. This is also true. It is the conclusion that is illogical.

This means Socrates is a man. This is a true statement. However, just because Socrates is mortal does not mean he is a man. All animals are also mortal. Based on the information that the premises provide, you cannot automatically assume that Socrates is a man.

There are also inductive arguments. However, when trying to apply critical thinking to an argument while thinking like a lawyer, these are not the best because they are based on assumptions.

The following is an inductive argument about the diets of Greeks.

Most Greeks eat fish.

Socrates is Greek.

Socrates eats fish.

This argument is inductive because you are using reasoning to figure out what kind of food Socrates would have eaten. Inductive means inferring general laws based on particular instances. We can assume that since Greeks rely heavily on fish for nutrients, Socrates would eat fish. When making an inductive argument, there are weak and strong arguments, and they are not going to be absolute. There will always be an outlier.

So, we have seen a good argument and a bad argument. Now we can talk about what not to include in your argument along with what an argument is *not*.

- Assertions: A confident, forceful statement of fact or belief. The key part of this definition is belief. This allows for opinions to be involved. While there are different types of arguments, you should understand that in this case, we need to argue facts. For example, saying that Muslims are bad is not an argument. It is a statement that would need to be supported by facts, or in our case, premises. It is also a belief.

- Statements: Einstein said, "God does not play dice with the universe." Is Einstein an intelligent human? Yes. Does this mean we should listen to everything he says and use it in a literal sense? No.

- Explanations: Because Caesar's army was outnumbered, they retreated across the Rhine. This is true, but it is not arguing anything. In fact, there is nothing here to argue.

- Opinions: Cannot stress this enough! Leave your opinions and emotions out of the picture!

A good argument will not include statements, and it will not attack the person making the opposing argument. This is called *ad hominem*. To combat *ad hominem*, you should refrain from involving emotions and disallow them from swaying your argument. *Ad hominem* can also be applied to assigning guilt due to association.

Let's expand upon the cognitive biases and talk about a few other things that can affect your argument and how it stands up against the arguments of others. For example, saying that one restaurant is better than another because your favourite celebrity is on the commercials does not make it a sound or valid argument. The celebrity does not determine the taste of the food or the speed of the service at the restaurant.

Appealing to pity is a good persuasive technique, but to create an argument that will stand on its own, you need factual information. So avoid the appeal to pity as one of your main points. When you are appealing to pity, often a visual aid is required to create the impact you are looking for.

When creating an argument, first you should rely on cold, hard facts. This is where statistics come in handy. Using statistics can create the same effect that visuals can, but there is only one way to interpret them. We often see the appeal to pity in propaganda. The same can be said about an appeal to fear. Any threats that include a threat to someone's life or someone's freedom should not be considered the main point. These can be utilized as supporting details, but ending your argument with threats will not result in a valid argument. If you are arguing that something must be good since there is no evidence to oppose or validate the argument, and thus an argument cannot be made, then don't try to make one. For example, let's say that you decided to argue that cotton must be good for you since there is no research stating otherwise you would not be correct. This is known as the appeal to ignorance.

Other things to consider when creating an argument include sweeping generalizations and selective observation. Sweeping generalizations occur when you take one instance and apply it to all situations. For example, you should never lie. However, if someone arrived at your house with a gun and asked if you had any children, what would you say? Lying and saying no could protect the lives of your children. In this case, telling the truth could put them in danger.

Selective observation is the act of only seeing information that will support your argument. When you use this in your argument, you allow the opposer to find the holes in your argument very easily which makes for a weak argument. Wishful thinking can also affect your argument. Remember, just because you wish for something to be true, does not mean it is. For example, let's say that you put your plastic and paper product in separate containers so that the trash disposal will recycle them. You say you are helping the environment, but really the company puts your recyclables in with the rest of the garbage. You are only seeing the part of the process that is supporting your belief that you are helping the environment.

In addition, just because the argument you want to make is not the most popular argument, it can still be sound, and by making your argument strong, people may actually learn that it is a better argument. For example, school uniforms are somewhat controversial. However, in recent times, many schools have switched over to uniforms due to the practicality. Do not allow the opinions of others sway your own. You should make observations, do research, and draw conclusions on your own. By doing this, you will be able to make your argument more convincing because while it is factual, you also believe it.

The example of an invalid argument uses circular reasoning because only one of the premises assumes the conclusions. All evidence must be included in your argument to come to the most logical conclusion. You should also focus on keeping your argument consistent. When researching, you should find multiple dependable sources that share consistent information. The more support your argument has, the stronger it will be.

In addition, remember that two wrongs do not make a right. For example, Allan's mother shot her husband because he beat her every night. Allan's mother is not justified because there are other ways to solve her problem. Quoting out of context is also not okay when trying to make a strong argument. Sure, you don't have to quote entire books word for word, but you should consider all of the information a source provides instead of just the information that supports your stance. You should consider this when using quotes. Do not cut off a quote before the "but" comes. If there is a "but" and you ignore it, your argument will be weakened.

Chapter 9
Critical Thinking Writing: 4 Steps For Perfect Critical Thinking Writing And Evaluation

Success in analytic cerebration autograph awaits on one's adeptness to compassionate aboriginal arguments, as able-bodied as interpreting them in differing credibility of views. You use altered credibility of angle to appraise worthiness, truthfulness, carefulness and acceptability of aboriginal arguments. Success in analytic cerebration autograph await on one's adeptness to compassionate aboriginal arguments, as able-bodied as interpreting them in differing credibility of views.

You use altered credibility of angle to appraise worthiness, truthfulness, carefulness and acceptability of aboriginal arguments. Success in analytic cerebration autograph awaits on one's adeptness to compassionate aboriginal arguments, as able-bodied as interpreting them in differing credibility of views. You use altered credibility of angle to appraise worthiness, truthfulness, carefulness and acceptability of aboriginal arguments.

Not alone is analytic cerebration accessible for success in bookish autograph and appointment writing, but additionally is an accomplishment actual accessible in accepted living. Issue is; you cannot accede to or acquire aggregate said or brought advanced by anyone anytime, alike in absolute life. A must-have action is developing important analytic acumen about any allotment of assignment or thing.

You charge acquaintance of assorted issues while criticizing any allotment of work. Here are accomplish you can use to finer absolute your analytic account for any allotment of work; 1. Assay the author's capital band of reasoning. In analytic cerebration writing, identification of this band of acumen has to do with assurance of the author's capital argument.

Whenever you appoint in analytic cerebration writing, ask what point of appearance an accurate columnist adopts. In some cases, you may accept to assay the credibility or positions authors avert a lot in their writing. In added cases, you may charge to attending at the case they abutment and for which they accommodate evidence.

You may accept to alpha analytic cerebration autograph by account an array of works or materials, either to accept an all-embracing compassionate of affairs originally aloft by author, or to assay the opposing credibility of angle from a cardinal of added authors. It is not accessible to accept an already taken point of appearance in analytic thinking: you can accession aboriginal opposing credibility of appearance as continued as affirmation exists.

Criticize the band of reasoning. Successful analytic cerebration autograph involves analytic appraisal of aboriginal curve of thoughts through an accurate strategy; to aboriginal attending at the aboriginal advice or ideas, assay them based on an assertive criteria, assay with facts on the ground, agenda flaws in arguments and processes of acumen and accession opposing account accurate by evidence. You charge to admission whether the affidavit accustomed to the aboriginal author's point of appearance is relevant. In analytic cerebration writing, acquisition out whether contributions accept acceptable propositions.

In addition, you charge to analysis if arguments are logical. For instance, if the columnist abiding account in capacity and subsections, you may analysis if account in anniversary of the capacity are analytic and fluent. Analytic cerebration autograph involves identification of; flaws in reasoning, flaws in appraisal and analytic procedures employed, flaws in presentation of abstracts and flaws in conclusions, as able-bodied as errors in a blueprint and their statement.

Assay if arguments await on truth/facts or if they are prejudices. Critical cerebration involves appraisal of whether arguments are accurate and whether they are bald prejudices. Valuable statements charge awaits on accuracy and is chargeless of prejudices.

Ensure to catechism apparent appearances Aboriginal authors charge assay affirmation for positions captivated or opinions posited. One abiding way of criticizing such an assignment in analytic celebration is allegoric attention of such evidence. Analytic cerebration autograph additionally involves allegory authority of affirmation in affiliation to dates and representation (for example, candour or abridgement of it).

Writing Critically and Writing A Clear Argument

Writing critically is very important in academic writing. In your English classes, you will be asked to write at least one argumentative paper that will ask you to defend one side or another. Critical writing can be broken down. To put it simply, critical writing evaluates and analyzes more than one source in order to develop an argument. This is different than descriptive writing which describes what something is like. However, description will be involved in your critical writing along with an explanation. There should be a good balance between analysis and description. Critical thinking will make your writing clearer and more concise. This allows you to make well-thought-out arguments in a shorter amount of time with more success. Being clear will increase readability. This will allow for a wider audience and a more enjoyable read. When writing, sometimes it is difficult to put your thoughts on paper without sounding crazy. Being told to write more clearly is a lot easier than actually writing clearly. Therefore, this is going to give you a few tips and pointers on becoming a better writer.

At this point, you have heard a lot about how to think critically, cognitive biases, and how to escape the trap Groupthink creates. Now, you will be able to write critically. When you are writing critically, you'll be able to word your thoughts better, and your paragraphs will be more useful – it won't just be about word counts anymore, but the word counts will be met regardless.

The following is a series of questions you can ask. These can be applied to writing and editing your writing:

Is your idea/argument a good or bad one?

Is my argument valid and defensible? Is it the opposite?

We have talked about how to determine whether an argument is valid, but you also need to be able to defend your argument with premises and supporting details. If you cannot do this, your point of view will be easy to poke holes in and will collapse like a house of cards.

Is my position on the issue rational and reasonable?

Reason is something we have already talked about quite a bit. It is important because it will justify your position.

Do I deal with the complexity of the situation or do I only utilize clichés and stereotypes to make my point?

Stereotypes are not foolproof; therefore, they should not be used in an argument because there are many instances where they will not be true. The same goes for clichés. Clichés are overused and only occur in a perfect situation.

Do I touch deeper points, or do I only scrape the surface when talking about my topic?

Go into detail! Details are so important, and the more valid support you have for your argument, the better. Don't be repetitive, but present as many different details as you can, especially in the first draft of your writing. You should strive to understand what you are writing about and encourage your readers to understand what they are reading.

Do I address the other points of view properly?

Always consider the counterarguments. These are going to test your own viewpoint, and those who support the counterarguments are going to be looking for things that will take your argument down.

Do I question my own ideas and test them for validity?

Question all of the evidence you find and make sure it is supported by things like experiments and observation. If there are surveys involved in your argument, make sure the pool of people surveyed is an accurate proportion.

Do I have specific goals in mind with this piece?

Create a goal and write it down. This will help you stick with the purpose of your argument.

When forming an argument and writing about it, you are going to need to give yourself time and be very organized. Your first step should be to research. Utilize all outlets that you have access to. Go to the library and read as much as you can about your topic first and write down important points and supporting details. Then, if you have access to any online databases, use those. Generally, depending on your topic, you will find statistics and experiments. Do not disregard anything because it does not directly address your viewpoint. Anything you can learn is good. The more you broaden your knowledge on the topic, the easier it will be for you to argue one way or another. You never know – halfway through, you may discover that you actually think the opposing viewpoint is better. Once you have searched databases, go to the search engines, and you will find the opinions of others and some more supporting details. The more information that you have and know about a topic, the easier your thoughts will flow. At this point, you should have several more sources than what is required. By the end, you will have to cut down the number of sources because you should not need them all.

Next, you should make outlines. That's right, multiple. Each should get more detailed, and by the end, you will have a sentence outline. This is essentially your first draft with different numbers and sections. You may think that making multiple outlines is excessive, but it will allow you to see your information in several different ways. When you look at an information in the same font in block paragraphs, it is difficult to determine whether or not it will be clear to readers. This is why having someone else edit it is important. Furthermore, if you don't have someone else, as long as you have given yourself enough time, you can put the project away and look at it the next day.

Your writing should not be confusing or full of hidden meaning. Make it as clear as possible. When you go through and edit, you should determine whether the following questions are easily found:

Is the purpose of the piece clear and easily found?

Stating the purpose in the first paragraph is the easiest way to do this. You are not trying to conceal your topic. There is no harm in including it in some of your first thoughts.

What questions does this piece answer? What questions are explored?

From what perspective is my argument?

You should know this for a couple of different reasons. Understanding your own perspective will allow you to write about it clearer. It will also allow you to determine the opposing viewpoints and determine counterarguments.

Where did I get my information? Are the sources valid? Was the information consistent in all of my sources?

What concepts are central in my line of thinking?

These would be your main points, a common number of main points is three, but you can have any number of main points to support your argument. These main points will have supporting details. They can be considered the premises of your arguments..

What conclusions am I making? What premises do I include?

These, of course, would be your entire argument. If you use a thesis statement, which you should, your premises and your conclusions will be found here. Your thesis statement will only feature your premises and your conclusion. Write the premises in the order that they will appear to make the thesis statement more usable.

Am I making any assumption/s? Are these assumptions that I should be making?

There is a difference between making an educated inference and just making assumptions. For example, if there are no clouds in the sky, we can assume it is not going to rain. However, just because George Clooney is not your father does not mean you can assume he is your best friend's father. You must have evidence to support this.

As a writer who writes critically, you should be able to evaluate your work thoroughly. The questions above will help you with this. While you write, you will use several different levels of thinking: validity, context, accuracy, and precision. The conclusions you make should be predictable when paired with all of the evidence you gathered. Always keep your argument reasonable, solid, and valid. In addition, you should always consider any weaknesses your argument has along with potential counterarguments. How does considering counterarguments help you? Well, you will be able to strengthen your own argument by pointing out the weaknesses in the counterarguments. You can also block the holes in your own argument by strategizing and using critical thinking. Make your weaknesses seem like strengths in an argument.

Writing is important and can help you think critically successfully. Writing requires you to do two things: write out your thoughts completely and make them readable to a varied audience. Thinking critically is like speaking proper English to someone who learned it as a second language. You may be introducing a concept completely new to your audience. This requires you to be extremely thorough, and you must know your topic completely. Your awareness of a topic will increase when you write it out, and complex problems can be worked through and solved.

Here are five steps that will aid you in the process of gathering evidence:

- Question everything and actively try to find new information. Examine, parse, and validate every piece of information you plan to utilize in your argument.

- Don't jump to conclusions or make assumptions. Come to a conclusion based on the evidence you have and not the evidence you don't have. In addition, you should determine whether or not your argument is too general. Are there other explanations?

- Keep your writing from repeating itself. When making an argument, redundancy can take over and weaken your argument. This is why it is so important to find as much information as you can. In addition, avoid truisms or self-evident truths.

- Do not oversimplify things. Use detailed explanations that go into depth.

- Find the holes in all arguments, including your own.

How do you determine if your writing is poor?

- The thesis is repetitive and does not indicate where the rest of the writing will lead. You are trying to write an informative, argumentative piece, not a mystery. Keep it clear all the way through.

- If you rely on simple summaries instead of explanations that have a lot of details, it is likely that there is not enough evidence to support your argument. This makes for a weak argument that is vague and lacks readability because things are not thoroughly explained. When talking about relationships between concepts, explain why they exist instead of stating that they exist.

- If your argument is disorganized, the reader will be able to tell. Disorganization is bad. It muddies the purpose and makes the argument unclear. Make sure everything is well-ordered. If you are explaining a step-by-step process, you need to make sure the steps are in order. If you utilize historical references, make sure that they are ordered chronologically.

- If you present ideas but not their relation to the argument, you are doing it wrong. Explanations are important! People are reading this so that they can understand your point of view!

- If your conclusions are not supported by your premises, your writing is not only bad, but your argument is also invalid. If your premises are incorrect, your conclusions are invalid.

- You use several sources and attempt to string their ideas together without actually analyzing what is being said. You must analyze what is being said instead of accepting it to be true.

Another important part of critical writing is the revision process. Revisions will not only refine your writing but are also intended to make your piece clearer. To make your argument better, play the devil's advocate. Present the article to yourself and decide what you would say to combat your own argument. Then, fill in the holes in your own argument. Repeat the revision process as many times as you can.

You can also look at your argument in different forms. This will help you see different strengths and weakness along with more ways to expand your argument. Review the evidence you found, depending on the argument. New evidence will likely come up. Using new evidence will strengthen your argument if it supports it. If a new argument that counters yours is discovered, you need to be able to combat this evidence and figure out how it will affect your point of view. The revision process will help you add to your argument, sure, but it will also help you remove the clutter or arguments that are no longer valid. If this argument is being made over a long period of time, you must constantly be revising your article. Pay attention to the start and end dates of your project to make sure you are as accurate as possible.

Find someone who has the opposing argument. Sometimes, in school, your instructor will assign someone to an opposing viewpoint. If possible, collaborate and use each other to strengthen your argument. This will also save you both some time because you can do your own research and come together. Hearing a voice other than your own can help you in several different ways. They can push your arguments to the limit, which will require you to re-evaluate your argument. You can also see if your words make sense coming from someone else or if your point of view has any cognitive biases present.

Lastly, in a best-case scenario, the critical thinker you shared your piece with reaches the same conclusions you did base on the premises you provided, and your argument is solid. During this process, always be as aware as possible and stay open-minded. Being faithful to your position in an argument is important and so is being open to other possibilities.

Chapter 10
Critical Thinking: Obstacles

Like most skills, anyone can develop critical thinking. But far from everyone can do it easily. Often on the way, there are all kinds of barriers and obstacles that impede the process. However, this should not stop you, because all of them can be overcome.

So what can stop you?

Reassessing Your Ability to Reason

Most people consider themselves as rational people and do not doubt the correctness and truth of their belief system, otherwise, they would simply not believe in what they believe. People are sure that they have knowledge and good reasons to act in a certain way.

But, despite the fact that this state of affairs concerns many of us, we often behave completely differently, because almost always think automatically. This is quite normal because this method is best suited for everyday life - putting on gloves or picking up a comb in our hands, we should not doubt that it is safe.

However, thinking this way, you can form bad habits with regards to thoughts and actions. Everyone who follows the path of least resistance will be confident in their true. But, prevailing in disputes, you can easily overestimate your ability to reason.

The ability to emerge victorious in a dispute does not at all guarantee the ability to operate with the best evidence. The dispute can be won due to the fact that the interlocutor could not recognize unconvincing arguments or simply decided to avoid confrontation.

Do not overestimate yourself: the lack of logic, inaccuracy and uncertainty only interfere with the development of critical thinking and abilities that allow you to professionally and competently communicate, work and learn.

Unwillingness to Critique

Excitement in situations where you need to look at things critically is quite natural. But he does not need to give in. For example, in many educational institutions, criticism is part of the learning process, as an everyday exercise. Here you just need to understand that you can adapt to critical thinking only over time.

Invalid Criticism Rating

Someone may think that criticism is a negative reaction, and when analyzing it, only negative aspects are taken into account. But in reality, criticism is also a definition of positive aspects, as well as effective and ineffective arguments.

Most people do not welcome criticism, because, in fact, this is a process with negative colouring. In the same way, many people try not to criticize, because they are afraid to create a reputation for themselves as not a very pleasant person.

The result is the avoidance of any kind of comments that the addressee may perceive as negative, and only positive ones are voiced. But this path does not lead to improvements and is unproductive. Only constructive criticism can lead to progress, improvement, and problem solving.

Lack of Practice, Strategies and Methods

Even developing critical thinking, many people do not understand what exactly needs to be done for this. The same skills that you have successfully used in school or communicating with friends may not be suitable for the professional field or for studying at a university. But you can learn everything, you just need to perform actions, and useful information will come as you study the theory.

The Impact of Emotions

One of the most important roles in the development of critical thinking is self-control. To think critically is to acknowledge the existence of more than one point of view on a problem. With regard to the areas of work and training, the use of theory in practice can cause controversy in a person if knowledge goes against his fundamental beliefs. And accepting this can be very difficult.

Most often this happens when an educated person or some kind of scientific research casts doubt on what everyone considers "common sense". And when a person is concerned about what he is interested in, emotions in some cases can give his thoughts the right direction, but more often they negatively affect the ability to think clearly.

The emotional component is capable of both giving facts and evidence strength and completely depriving them of it. In particular, this happens when emotional arguments are at the forefront that can convince the other person.

Critical thinking requires a person to drop everything that he believes and considers as important. You can safely say that to think critically is to select as carefully as possible information that supports arguments and statements without giving them an emotional colouring. Only in this way can one reasonably argue one's position.

Inattention to Detail and Lack of Concentration

As you already know, critical thinking implies accuracy and accuracy, and this is directly related to attention to detail. If your idea of the topic of conversation, problem or subject is too general, then the judgments will be superficial, and criticism will be ineffective. Thinking critically means fully focusing on a problem. Here it should be noted that when evaluating an argument, you need to remember that it can be objective and correct, even if your opinion is completely different.

Misunderstanding

The development of critical thinking requires the development of the ability to understand and understand the essence of things. But some people prefer blind trust in facts and ready-made answers, neglecting the development of self-judgment and information.

Of course, a competent approach requires effort and time, but if critical thinking were easy, no one would have learned to use this skill in life, work and training. With effort, you train your brain, making it more flexible and stronger.

Conformism and Propaganda

The desire to be like others is one of the most serious barriers to the development of critical thinking. People are often afraid to express ideas and opinions that are different from those generally accepted, being afraid to seem stupid or funny. This also includes the values instilled in society by culture, politics, show business, and the media.

But to think critically is to think independently, without adapting to someone, without being guided by what others think. Public opinion is a very changeable thing, and to go against it you need to be a big daredevil. But this is precisely your task - to learn to think outside the box, as if abstracting from what is being imposed by society, trusting only what has been personally tested by you on experience.

Censorship

Censorship is a logical continuation of the previous paragraph. But if before that it was a question of external influences, then we need to attach importance to what is inside. Of course, if you go against external censorship, you can come to negative consequences, but it is the internal borders that are the most difficult to deal with.

Constraining internal attitudes and beliefs lead to fear of one's own ideas, a passive reaction to the surrounding reality, the inability to critically evaluate the incoming data, and the lack of a creative approach to solving problems.

Instant Result

Often critical thinking is hindered by the banal desire to achieve results immediately - right now. Because of too high motivation, people often make inadequate and thoughtless decisions, seeking as soon as possible to find a way out or implement their plan. And this approach is ineffective, because Forces to rely on unverified and unconfirmed information.

The best way out of this situation is to maintain calm, rationality, understanding that rushing will not lead to anything good. Critical thinking will be effective only when you develop the habit of weighing facts, considering them from different angles, and experimenting. And, as you yourself understand, acting in haste with this approach is unacceptable.

Cognitive Distortion

It has long been known that human perception is associated with his thinking and judgments, which he makes on the subject of any phenomenon, fact or event. But thinking is far from always a reflection of reality, and in it one can track various deviations and errors, including systematic ones.

Cognitive distortions can be a consequence of the influence of society, emotional and moral factors, limited brain capabilities, impaired data processing and mental noise. But these distortions can be controlled and corrected using special techniques.

If you encounter cognitive biases, it is best to contact a psychologist to help solve this problem.

Problem Solving Exercises to Boost Critical Thinking Skills

Exercise 1: "To-Do" Scavenger Hunt

This is best done in a group of people, such as in a classroom or with other people around. You must set up a series of challenges that are then expected to be done in groups, allowing everyone to work toward the same end goal. When you do this, try to start out with groups of people and randomized tasks, but if you are by yourself, you can also do so by setting up several dozen random problem-solving exercises and then drawing out six every time you challenge yourself to this. Each of the problems that are included should be something relatively simple but will require you to work with some sort of problem solving.

For example, maybe you challenge yourself to write a poem about one specific theme. This theme could be anything at random, and it has to rhyme, with the first of the words provided for you. Perhaps the first line of the poem must end in "Yellow," and every other line must rhyme with it, all about the topic of winter.

Another example could bet to drink an entire glass of liquid without spilling it—without your hands and without a straw.

You then need to figure out a way to allow yourself to drink that glass without touching it.

As you can see, the problems that must be solved do not need to be serious problems—making them into games can actually make the problem-solving that much more enjoyable. When you do this, you can encourage yourself to think outside of the box in low-stakes environments. As a bonus, if you do this in a group, it can be fun to watch people try to solve these lists together!

Exercise 2: Will it Float?

In this exercise, you and a group of people, if you have anyone around that can help you with this, are tasked with coming up with some sort of float with only the items that you can get your hands on in 30 seconds. When you are ready to begin, someone sets off a 30-second timer, and everyone is off to gather their ingredients. The task at hand is to create some sort of raft that will allow for a paperclip to float atop a body of water. The teams or groups are given 5 minutes to complete the challenge before competing.

This particular exercise brings two skills to the table: Not only you require yourself to think critically, you are also forcing yourself to work in a team as well. This means that you have to use several other critical thinking skills, such as communicating well and making sure that you are listening to all suggestions in the race.

Exercise 3: A Marble Run—with a Twist

In this exercise, you are challenged to come up with a marble run. If you have children, you may already have a kit for this. However, you need to set up a marble run that is able to trigger something. Your marble run must be used to put out a candle that is sitting on a table. Of course, you must be mindful of danger when doing this—make sure that you are using your own fire safety skills and do not burn down the room that you are doing the challenge in. However, beyond that, the only limit here is your imagination.

When you do this challenge, you must figure out how to use a marble run to trigger a reaction that will extinguish a candle. There are several different ways you could do this—you could have a cup fall upside-down over the candle to make the candle go out. You could try having water spilled on the candle at the end of the marble run, or you could even use the marble run to turn on a fan that blows it out. No matter the method that you choose, however, it only counts if you are able to drop the marble in the beginning and have the candle blown out. Good luck!

This is meant to make you start thinking both critically and creatively—you have a task at hand in blowing out the candle somehow, and you have a method to do so—using a marble run. How can you, or even a group of people, figure out how best to use the marble run to trigger the candle to go out? This can be tricky to figure out at first, but once you do it, you will find that marble runs, despite being aimed toward children, can be quite fun.

Exercise 4: The Spaghetti Bridge

Perhaps done with your children when working on teaching them critical thinking as well, this last exercise is to make some sort of bridge using straight spaghetti noodles and anything else that you can find to create a bridge that will stand while small die-cast cars are driven over it. The trick here is to ensure that the bridge is able to withstand the weight while still standing.

Particularly for children, this can be exciting—dry pasta is not exactly notorious for being particularly difficult to snap. Nevertheless, when you use this method, you are working together to figure out how to solve the problem, and having fun while you do it.

Conclusion

Thank you for reading through this book. The next step is to make your choices with confidence. We really hope that you are able to think for yourself, and make choices that reflect that.

This book is meant to show you that you can think for yourself, and make choices that only you agree with. The more you put these things to use, the easier it is going to be to make these choices on your own, and to stick with them.

Independence is a beautiful thing, and the better you get at critical thinking, the more you are going to become your own person. It is an odd thing, thinking that you are not your own person, but until you are able to take a hold of your life and think in your own functioning manner, you are not going to be independent.

If you are serious about making your own decisions, and thinking not only about things, but also thinking through them, you are going to find that the lessons in this book are for you.

We want you to be confident in your decisions, and make choices that you feel are right for you, even if no one else is doing it. You are able to think for yourself, and that is something that is going to serve you well in your life, for life.

You have a brain that works virtually like a supercomputer. It is that brain that directs the way your body functions, and it is the same brain that determines how you tailor your life. It also has a great influence on who you are as an individual, what you actually do and even the proficiency with which you do it.

For that reason, it is very important that you maintain the health of your brain, because, in so doing, you are going to be better at decision-making. You will also be better placed to think logically, and to do things that have a positive impact on your life. Mark you, it does not mean that when you think in a logical manner you erode your emotions. It only means that you are able to let reason prevail over your feelings, making decisions that can be easily validated.

It is important to bear in mind the fact that your own brain is unique, and that it is more complicated than even that supercomputer you have read about. In all ways, your brain happens to be one amazing organ whose health you cannot afford to ignore. You need to be protective of it, particularly seeing to it that it does not lose its elasticity. If your brain lost its elasticity, you would find yourself becoming complacent, and as you may guess, complacency is a poor ingredient in the process of critical thinking.

The advantage you have now is that you have learned from this book what you need to do in terms of exercises, in order to keep your brain elastic and working in a logical manner. And, as you have also seen, consistency is the way to go – engaging in critical thinking at every opportune moment.

All the best, as you seek to improve your life through critical thinking!

www.ingramcontent.com/pod-product-compliance
Lightning Source LLC
Chambersburg PA
CBHW070637220526
45466CB00001B/204